LONG-TERM PROJECTS

Algebra 2

HOLT, RINEHART AND WINSTON

A Harcourt Classroom Education Company

Austin · New York · Orlando · Atlanta · San Francisco · Boston · Dallas · Toronto · London

To the Teacher

Long-Term Projects contains blackline masters that complement regular classroom use of *Algebra 2*. These projects are especially helpful in accommodating students of varying interests, learning styles, and ability levels. There is one four-page Long-Term Project for each chapter of *Algebra 2*. These projects engage students in activities that encompass more than one class period. Projects often require data collection or research to be done outside the classroom. Many of the projects are appropriate for group work.

Photo Credit
Front Cover: Tom Paiva/FPG International.

Printed in the United States of America

ISBN 0-03-054083-6

6 7 8 9 10 11 023 08 07 06 05 04

Table of Contents

Long-Term Project

Stock Market Analysis, Chapter 1

During one week in March of 1998, the Dow Jones 30 Industrials set a new record high each day. The averages, to the nearest whole point, for those days are recorded in the table below.

Day	1	2	3	4	5
Dow Jones Average	8719	8750	8775	8803	8906

In Exercises 1–6, refer to the table above.

1. Label the vertical axis so that all of the data can be plotted on the grid at right. Notice that the vertical axis shows a break.

2. Plot each of the ordered pairs from the table on the grid. Then make a broken line graph by connecting each point with the next.

3. Describe the overall trend seen in the broken-line graph.

   _____

   _____

4. **a.** On your graph, draw the line segment whose endpoints are (1, 8719) and (5, 8906).

   b. Find the slope of that line segment.

   _____

   c. Interpret the slope from part **b** as a rate of change. _____

   d. Using the slope from part **b** and one of the endpoints of the segment, write an equation in slope-intercept form for the line containing those

      points. _____

5. Use your equation from part **d** of Exercise 4 to predict p given each value of d.

   a. 10 _____   **b.** 15 _____   **c.** 20 _____   **d.** 25 _____

6. Is the model you found in part **d** of Exercise 4 a good long-term model? Explain.

   _____

   _____

Long-Term Project

Stock Market Analysis, Chapter 1, page 2

The stock market data you explored on the preceding page is reproduced here.

Day	1	2	3	4	5
Dow Jones Average	8719	8750	8775	8803	8906

In Exercises 7–12, use a graphics calculator and your answers to Exercises 1–6.

7. Enter the data in the table into a graphics calculator. Find an equation for the least-squares line. Give your coefficients rounded to the nearest tenth of a unit.

   _____

8. Using your equation from Exercise 7, predict p given each value of d.

   a. 10 _____   **b.** 15 _____   **c.** 20 _____   **d.** 25 _____

9. How do your answers to Exercise 8 compare with those from Exercise 5?

   _____

   _____

10. Is the model you found in Exercise 7 a good long-term model? Explain.

    _____

    _____

11. **a.** Find the correlation coefficient for the variables d and p. _____

    b. Explain why a high correlation coefficient does not always tell you that an equation is a good long-term model of data.

    _____

    _____

12. Evaluate the data in terms of its acceptability as a good sample for stock market analysis.

    _____

    _____

Long-Term Project

Stock Market Analysis, Chapter 1, page 3

The table below contains Nasdaq Index data along with the Dow Jones data.

Day	1	2	3	4	5
Dow Jones Average	8719	8750	8775	8803	8906
Nasdaq Index	38	41	46	39	36

13. Find the rate of change in the Nasdaq data by finding the slope of the line containing (1, 38) and (5, 36). _____

14. Does the Nasdaq Index data show the same overall trend as the Dow Jones data? Explain.

_____

15. Miguel argued that the Nasdaq data shows a downward trend.

  a. Find an equation for the least-squares line for the Nasdaq data. Give your coefficients rounded to the nearest tenth of a unit. _____

  b. Find the correlation coefficient. _____

  c. Do the equation and the correlation coefficient from parts **a** and **b** support Miguel's view? Explain.

_____

16. Using your equation from part **a** of Exercise 15, predict p given each value of d.

  a. 10 _____ **b.** 15 _____ **c.** 20 _____ **d.** 25 _____

17. What conclusions can you draw when you compare the answers to parts **a–d** from Exercise 16 with the corresponding answers from Exercise 8?

_____

18. What happens if you apply the rate of change found in part **c** of Exercise 4 and the rate of change you found in Exercise 13 over a fourteen-day period starting with day 1?

_____

19. a. What can you conclude about the stock market when you analyze your calculations from Exercise 18?

_____

  b. What can you conclude from the least-squares line and correlation coefficients for the Dow Jones data when compared to the same mathematical calculations for the Nasdaq data?

_____

Long-Term Project
Stock Market Analysis, Chapter 1, page 4

This table gives the High, Low, Close, and Change for various Dow Jones Indices for a day in April 1998.

	High	Low	Close	Change
30 Industrials	9206.36	8983.65	9064.62	−78.71
20 Transports	3658.18	3527.73	3558.02	−73.07
15 Utilities	283.82	278.17	280.00	−1.92
65 Stocks	2952.32	2872.76	2897.25	−34.44

One important indicator in analyzing the stock market is percent change.

In Exercises 20–21, you will set up an equation to calculate percent change.

20. **a.** Which items in the table are needed to calculate percent change? _____

   b. Choose variables to represent these items and a variable to represent percent change. Then write an equation using these variables.

_____

21. Use your equation to calculate the percent change, to the nearest hundredth, for each index.

22. Describe any relationships between the percent changes for the various Dow Jones indices for this day. How could you use this information to help you in investing?

_____

Index	Percent change
30 Industrials	
20 Transports	
15 Utilities	
65 Stocks	

_____

23. Look at the data for the High, Low, and Close for the Dow Jones Indices. Write a compound inequality that shows the relationship between the High, Low, and Close.

_____

24. The diagram at right shows the activity of one stock over the course of one day. On the grids below, sketch two other possible behaviors of a stock over the course of one day.

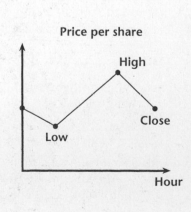

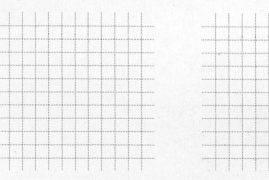

Long-Term Project

Objects in Orbit and Launching Vehicles, Chapter 2

In this project, you will explore objects in circular motion. Such objects obey physical laws that can be represented by equations.

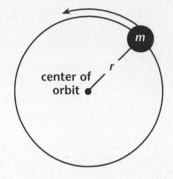

$$f_c = \frac{4\pi^2 mr}{T^2}$$

$\begin{cases} m \text{ represents the mass of the object in kilograms} \\ r \text{ represents the radius of the orbit in meters} \\ T \text{ represents the period of the orbit in seconds} \\ f_c \text{ represents the centripetal force in newtons} \end{cases}$

The equation above represents the relationship between centripetal force and the mass of an object, the radius of its orbit, and the time it takes for the object to make one complete revolution (the period of the orbit).

In Exercises 1 and 2, complete each table of values, giving values rounded to the nearest hundredth. Then tell, in general terms, how f_c changes as the specified variable changes.

1. An object has a mass of 2.5 kilograms. The object completes one orbit in 15 seconds.

r	1	2	3	4	5	6	7
f_c							

2. An object travels around an orbit that has a radius of 18 meters. The object makes one complete revolution in 55 seconds.

m	1	2	3	4	5	6	7
f_c							

3. Explain why the equation above represents a function. What restrictions are placed on its variables?

You can rewrite $f_c = \frac{4\pi^2 mr}{T^2}$ as $T = \sqrt{\frac{4\pi^2 mr}{f_c}}$.

4. A 10-kilogram object in a 3-meter orbit and a 3-kilogram object in a 10-meter orbit begin moving at the same time. Both objects have the same centripetal force. Which will complete a revolution first? Explain.

Long-Term Project

Objects in Orbit and Launching Vehicles, Chapter 2, page 2

You can compare the orbits of two objects in circular orbits about the same point. The equation below, known as *Kepler's Third Law*, gives a relationship between the two orbits.

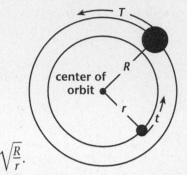

$$\frac{T^2}{t^2} = \frac{R^3}{r^3}$$

$\begin{cases} T \text{ represents the time needed for the first orbit} \\ R \text{ represents the radius of the first orbit} \\ t \text{ represents the time needed for the second orbit} \\ r \text{ represents the radius of the second orbit} \end{cases}$

5. You can rewrite the equation above as $T = \sqrt{\frac{t^2 R^3}{r^3}}$. Show that $T = \frac{tR}{r}\sqrt{\frac{R}{r}}$.

_____

In Exercises 6 and 7, the period of Earth's orbit is 1 year and the radius of that orbit is 9.30×10^7 miles. Compare the period of each planet to that of Earth. All orbit radii are in miles.

6. Venus, radius: 6.72×10^7 7. Mars, radius: 1.42×10^8

_____   _____

8. If $t = 1$ and $r = 9.30 \times 10^7$, then $T = \dfrac{1}{9.30 \times 10^7 \times \sqrt{9.30 \times 10^7}} R\sqrt{R}$.

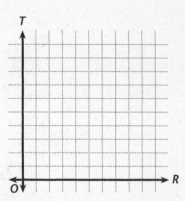

a. Use a calculator to simplify the fraction on the right side of the equation. Write your answer in scientific notation. Then write the function for T in simpler form.

_____

b. Use a graphics calculator to graph T as a function of R. Reproduce the general trend in your graph on the grid at right. Keep your graph in your graphics calculator.

c. From the graph, how does T change with R?

_____

9. Refer to your graphics calculator graph from part **b** in Exercise 8. Suppose an imaginary planet takes 1.5 Earth years to make one orbit around the Sun. Approximately what is the orbit's radius? _____

10. Based on an examination of the graph that shows T as a function of R, is the relationship that gives R in terms of T a function? That is, can you approximate the radius of the orbit of a planet if you know how long it takes for the planet to make one complete orbit? Explain your response.

_____

_____

Long-Term Project

Objects in Orbit and Launching Vehicles, Chapter 2, page 3

The diagram at right shows a primitive model of the external fuel tank used to take a space shuttle into outer space. The diagram shows a composite figure made up of a cone, a cylinder, and a hemisphere.

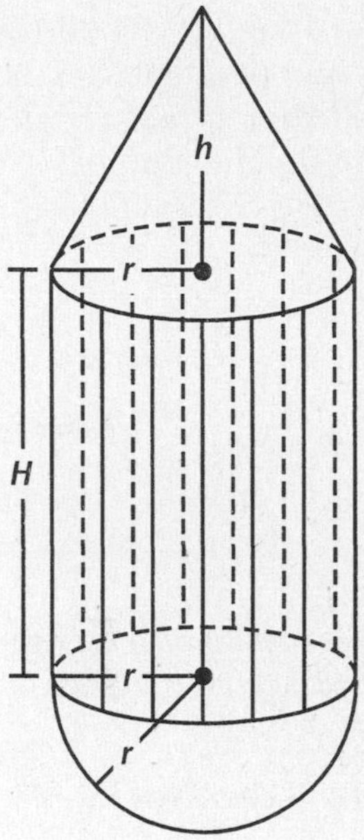

Let V_c represent the volume of the cone, V_s represent the volume of the cylinder, and V_h represent the volume of the hemisphere. Write volume functions for each section of the tank.

11. cone

12. cylinder

13. hemisphere

_____

_____

_____

14. Write a single function for the volume, V_f, of the entire tank. What function operation(s) did you use?

_____

15. Find the volume of the tank if the radius is 4.2 meters, the height of the cylinder is 21.2 meters, and the height of the cone is 8.1 meters. Round to the nearest hundredth of a cubic meter.

_____

Engineers are experimenting with different proportions for the specifications of the tank. Write a function for V_f given each relationship or relationships.

16. r as shown and $H = 6h$

17. r as shown, $H = 6r$, and $h = 1.5r$

_____

_____

18. Explain how composition of functions was involved in answering Exercises 16 and 17.

_____

One design that was rejected was the fuel tank shown above but with the hemispherical part inverted so that the hemisphere was nested inside the cylinder rather than protruding from it.

19. **a.** Let V_f represent the fuel capacity of the tank shown above and let V_i represent the fuel capacity of the rejected design for the tank. Write a function for $V_f - V_i$ in terms of r.

_____

    b. Explain how you arrived at the expression for $V_f - V_i$.

_____

    c. If the radius of the hemisphere is 4.2 meters, evaluate $V_f - V_i$. Round your answer to the nearest cubic meter.

_____

Long-Term Project

Objects in Orbit and Launching Vehicles, Chapter 2, page 4

In an effort to build a solar-system observation deck in space, engineers plan to launch tapered columns. One of them is shown at right. They plan to nest the columns as shown below. In the diagram below, s represents the distance between the larger bases of adjacent columns.

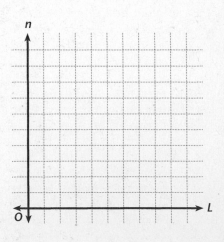

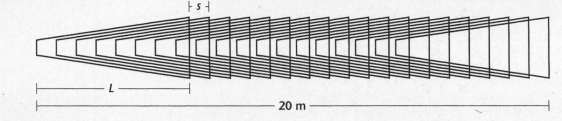

Engineers will want to know n, the number of nested columns that can fit into a space 20 meters long.

In Exercises 20–23, refer to the diagrams above.

20. a. Justify the inequality $L + (n - 1)s \leq 20$.

_____

   b. By solving the inequality in part **a** for n, justify the equation $n = \left[\dfrac{20 - L}{s} + 1 \right]$.

_____

21. a. Suppose that s equals 0.1 meters. Write the equation from part **b** of Exercise 20 as a function of L. _____

   b. Using a graphics calculator, graph the function from part **a**. Reproduce the general trend and shape on the grid at right. Describe the graph. How is it related to the graph of $y = [x]$?

_____

_____

The distance s is a function of the characteristics of the column. If a column has a thickness of t meters, then s can be approximated by $s = \dfrac{tL}{r_2 - r_1}$.

22. Analyze $s = \dfrac{tL}{r_2 - r_1}$ given that t, r_1, and r_2 are held constant.

_____

23. Given $t = 0.005$, $L = 5.000$, $r_2 = 0.055$, and $r_1 = 0.022$, how many columns will fit? _____

Long-Term Project

Using Systems of Equations to Analyze Nutrition, Chapter 3

Systems of linear equations and inequalities, along with linear programming, can help you analyze what you eat. In this project, you will investigate two important nutrients in your diet, calcium and iron. You will also see how the fat content of foods can be determined.

Calcium and iron are important elements for the development of strong bones and muscle tissue. The daily requirements of calcium and iron for 15–18-year-old males and females are shown in the table at right.

	Iron	Calcium
Male	12 milligrams	1200 milligrams
Female	12 milligrams	1500 milligrams

The table below shows the amounts of iron, calcium, and fat in a one-ounce serving of cereal and a one-ounce serving of whole milk.

	Iron	Calcium	Fat
Cereal (1 ounce)	4.51 milligrams	19.85 milligrams	0.65 grams
Whole milk (1 ounce)	0.03 milligrams	33.74 milligrams	0.94 grams

In Exercises 1–3, refer to the table above.

1. Let x represent the number of ounces of cereal and y represent the number of ounces of milk.

    a. Write an equation showing how to get your daily requirement of

    calcium if you eat only these two food items. _____

    b. Write an equation showing how to get your daily requirement of iron

    if you eat only these two food items. _____

2. Use a graphics calculator to find the intersection of the graphs of the equations that you wrote in parts **a** and **b** of Exercise 1.

    $x \approx$ _____ $y \approx$ _____

3. a. How much milk and how much cereal would you have to drink and eat to satisfy the daily minimum requirements for calcium and iron?   _____

    b. Is this a reasonable amount of milk and cereal to consume? Explain your answer.

    _____

    _____

    _____

    _____

Long-Term Project

Using Systems of Equations to Analyze Nutrition, Chapter 3, page 2

4. Suppose that you decide to get only 30% of your daily requirements of iron and calcium from these two foods. Write and solve a new system. Are these amounts of milk and cereal more reasonable for breakfast?

System: _____   Solution: _____

_____

The table below shows the amounts of iron and calcium in some other foods.

	Iron (milligrams)	Calcium (milligrams)	Fat (grams)
Tofu (1 ounce)	2.98	193.63	2.47
Orange juice (1 ounce)	0.06	3.12	0.06
Roast lamb (1 ounce)	0.62	2.27	2.61
Steak (1 ounce)	0.85	1.98	2.95
Chocolate ice cream	0.26	30.90	3.12
Swiss cheese	0.06	272.44	7.80

5. Choose two foods from this table. Assume that you will get 50% of your daily requirements from these two foods. Let x represent the number of ounces of the first food you chose and y represent the number of ounces of the second food you chose. Write a system of equations like the one you

wrote in Exercise 4. _____

6. Solve your system using the elimination method.

$x \approx$ _____ $y \approx$ _____

7. If you get 30% of your daily requirements from milk and cereal, and 50% from the foods you selected in Exercise 5, how could you get the rest of your daily requirements of calcium and iron?

_____

You have probably heard that it is important not to have too much fat in your diet. According to the American Heart Association, a daily diet should contain no more than 30% of calories from fat. The recommended daily intake of calories for males and females ages 15–18 is shown in the table at right.

	Calories
Male	3000
Female	2200

8. What is the maximum amount of calories from fat that is recommended by the American Heart Association?

_____

Long-Term Project

Using Systems of Equations to Analyze Nutrition, Chapter 3, page 3

9. A gram of fat takes 9 calories to burn. How many grams of fat would be equivalent to your answer in Exercise 8? _____

Suppose that you wanted to consume no more than $\frac{1}{3}$ of your fat allowance at each meal. If you are female, this means you could have a maximum of 24.4 grams of fat at breakfast.

In Exercises 10–12, consider the amount of fat that is contained in a breakfast of cereal and whole milk.

10. Write a function in two variables showing the total amount of fat, f, contained in x ounces of cereal and y ounces of milk.

_____

11. Write an inequality showing the amount of fat that has been allocated for breakfast. Graph the inequality.

_____

12. Choose a reasonable serving of these two items and determine how many fat grams you may consume for the rest of your day. Discuss how you could drink more milk and keep the fat grams to a minimum.

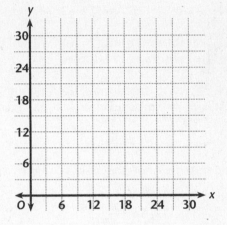

In Exercises 13 and 14, consider a fuller breakfast consisting of cereal, milk, and orange juice.

13. Write a function in three variables showing the total amount of fat, f, contained in x ounces of cereal, y ounces of milk, and z ounces of orange juice.

_____

14. Write an inequality showing that the amount of fat is less than 24.4 grams. Suppose that you have 6 ounces of orange juice. Graph the inequality.

_____

15. How much milk and cereal might you

consume? _____

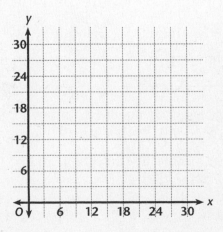

Long-Term Project

Using Systems of Equations to Analyze Nutrition, Chapter 3, page 4

You have been asked to prepare a nutritional dinner for a friend. You want to include roast lamb for the main dish and chocolate ice cream for dessert. You want to have at least 8 milligrams of iron and less than 200 milligrams of calcium.

16. Write two inequalities to model this situation.

_____

17. Graph the solution to the system on a graphics calculator. Draw a sketch on the grid at right.

You can use linear programming to minimize the fat in your servings of these two foods.

18. Write an objective function for the amount of fat contained in lamb and chocolate ice cream.

_____

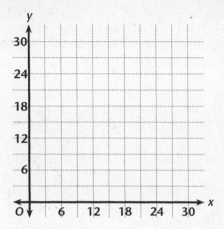

19. Find the number of ounces of lamb and ice cream that provides the minimal amount of fat.

_____

20. Discuss these portions in terms of your goal to have one-third of your fat allowance at each meal.

_____

Now your goal is to have at least 8 milligrams of iron and less than 200 milligrams of calcium from a combination of three foods rather than two foods.

21. a. Choose a third food, and write a new system of inequalities.

_____

b. Choose a fixed amount for one of the foods. Graph the system at right.

c. Write an objective function for the amount of total fat.

_____

d. How much of each food might you have?

_____

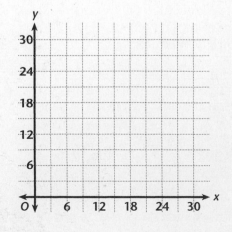

Long-Term Project

Matrices in an Amusement Park, Chapter 4

A group of friends went to an amusement park. They had just studied matrices in their algebra class, and they were interested in finding ways that matrices could be used to organize information.

The following tables show how many times each person rode each attraction, as well as the number of tickets required to ride.

	Roller coaster	Bumper cars	Ferris wheel	Fun house
Brett	3	4	2	3
Terri	5	2	0	1
George	0	5	4	0
Ondine	2	0	2	0

	Tickets required
Roller coaster	5
Bumper cars	3
Ferris wheel	2
Fun house	1

1. Write four separate 1×4 matrices to show the number of times that each person rode each attraction.

   a. Brett

   $B = \begin{bmatrix} \qquad\qquad\qquad \end{bmatrix}$

   b. Terri

   $T = \begin{bmatrix} \qquad\qquad\qquad \end{bmatrix}$

   c. George

   $G = \begin{bmatrix} \qquad\qquad\qquad \end{bmatrix}$

   d. Ondine

   $O = \begin{bmatrix} \qquad\qquad\qquad \end{bmatrix}$

2. Find the matrix $B + T + G + O$. Explain the meaning of each of the entries in the new matrix.

   $B + T + G + O = \begin{bmatrix} \qquad\qquad\qquad \end{bmatrix}$

   _____

3. Now write a single 4×4 matrix to show the number of times that each person rode each attraction. Call this matrix X.

   $X = \begin{bmatrix} \qquad\qquad\qquad \\ \\ \\ \end{bmatrix}$

4. Write a 4×1 matrix R to show the number of tickets required to ride each attraction.

   $R = \begin{bmatrix} \\ \\ \\ \end{bmatrix}$

Long-Term Project

Matrices in an Amusement Park, Chapter 4, page 2

5. Explain why it is possible to find XR, and give its dimensions.

_____

6. Find XR.

_____

7. For the matrix XR, explain the meaning of each of the matrix entries, if they exist.

   a. a_{11} _____

   b. a_{21} _____

   c. a_{22} _____

8. Each ticket costs \$2.00. Show how to use scalar multiplication to write a matrix showing how much each person spent on tickets.

_____

The floor plan of the fun house is shown in the diagram below. The arrows shown in each doorway indicate which way you are allowed to go through the door.

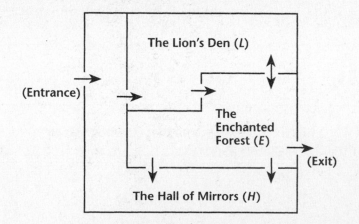

9. In the space at right, sketch a network diagram to represent this situation. Include one vertex for each room of the fun house, and include an additional vertex O representing the outside world.

NAME ______________________ CLASS ____________ DATE ____________

Long-Term Project

Matrices in an Amusement Park, Chapter 4, page 3

10. The matrix below is an adjacency matrix indicating how many one-stage paths are possible from one room in the fun house to another. (Think of the outside world as a "room.") Some of the entries have been determined for you. Fill in the remaining entries.

$$\begin{array}{rc} & \text{To:} \\ & \begin{array}{cccc} L & E & H & O \end{array} \\ \text{From:} \begin{array}{c} L \\ E \\ H \\ O \end{array} & \begin{bmatrix} & & 0 & \\ & & 2 & \\ & & 0 & \\ & & 1 & \end{bmatrix} \end{array}$$

11. If A is the matrix above, then the product $A \times A = A^2$ gives the number of 2-stage paths, which are from one room to another by means of one intermediate room. Calculate A^2.

____

12. How many 2-stage paths are there from the Lion's Den to the Hall of Mirrors?

____

13. Interpret n_{32} in the matrix. Describe or sketch the corresponding paths.

____

____

14. Design a fun house of your own, using at least three rooms and at least five doors. Sketch the floor plan of your fun house. Then find an adjacency matrix, A, describing your fun house, and calculate A^2. Interpret one of the entries in A^2, as you did in Exercise 13.

Fantastic Einstein offered to guess the heights and weights of the four friends. He guesses heights (in inches) and weights (in pounds) very scientifically. He asks for the height added to twice the weight, and then the weight plus twice the height.

His assistant uses a graphics calculator and inverse matrices to find the answer, which he whispers to Fantastic Einstein.

Long-Term Project

Matrices in an Amusement Park, Chapter 4, page 4

15. Brett gave the answers to the questions as 348 and 276 respectively. Write the system of equations that Fantastic Einstein's assistant used to find Brett's height and weight.

_____

_____

16. Solve this system using inverse matrices. _____

17. Terri gave the answers 313 and 251. Write and solve a new system

using inverse matrices. _____

18. Show the formula that the assistant uses by letting c represent the answer to the first question and d represent the answer to the second question. (Remember that the formula involves inverse matrices.)

_____

All together, Brett, George, and Ondine spent $142. Brett spent $6 less than George and Ondine combined. Brett spent $12 more than 2 times what Ondine spent.

19. Write and solve a system of equations using inverse matrices and your calculator. How much did each person spend?

_____

20. In the space below, show how to solve the system by using the row-reduction method. Your answers should match the amounts in Exercise 19.

21. On a separate sheet of paper, write your own word problem involving the amount of money spent by a group of three friends at an amusement park. Make sure that solving the problem involves a system of three linear equations. Show how to solve your problem using inverse matrices. Then show how to solve it using the row-reduction method.

_____

Long-Term Project

Fireworks and Quadratic Functions, Chapter 5

The heights of rockets in a Fourth of July fireworks show can be modeled by quadratic functions. In this project, you will use quadratic functions to help design your own fireworks show.

The quadratic function $h(t) = -16t^2 + v_0 t$ gives the altitude of an object launched from the surface of Earth.

$$\begin{cases} t: & \text{elapsed time in seconds} \\ v_0: & \text{initial upward velocity in feet per second} \\ h(t): & \text{altitude in feet} \end{cases}$$

The first rocket in the show will be launched with an upward velocity of 256 feet per second, so its height is given by $h(t) = -16t^2 + 256t$.

1. State whether the parabola represented by $h(t) = -16t^2 + 256t$ opens up or down. Explain why your answer makes sense.

_____

2. Graph $h(t) = -16t^2 + 256t$ on the grid at right. Begin by completing the table of values below.

t	0	4	8	12	16
$h(t)$					

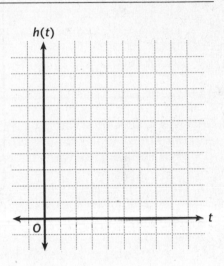

3. Use your graph to find the coordinates of the vertex of this function. Is the y-coordinate of the vertex the minimum value or the maximum value of the function?

_____

4. What do the coordinates of the vertex tell you about the flight of the rocket?

_____

5. Explain why negative values for t and $h(t)$ do not make sense for this problem.

_____

A sparkler display is to be dropped from a plane 1500 feet high immediately after the first rocket bursts. Neglecting air resistance, its altitude is given by $h(t) = -16t^2 + 1500$.

6. The display has a parachute that will be opened by a timer. If the timer does not work, when will the display hit the ground? Round your answer to the nearest tenth of a second. (Hint: Set $h(t)$ equal to 0.)

_____

Long-Term Project
Fireworks and Quadratic Functions, Chapter 5, page 2

7. You want the parachute to open when the sparkler package has an altitude of 600 feet. How much time should be put on the timer? Explain how you solved this problem.

_____

8. Graph $h(t) = -16t^2 + 1500$ on the grid at right. Complete the table below to help you.

t					
$h(t)$					

9. Use your graph to check your answers to Exercises 6 and 7. Explain how the graph confirms your answers.

_____

_____

_____

Fireworks in large shows are usually detonated by timed fuses. You must determine the detonation times for four of the rockets in the show. The first of the rockets will be launched with an initial upward velocity of 224 feet per second.

10. Write a quadratic function to represent the altitude of this rocket as a

function of elapsed time. _____

11. Set $h(t)$ equal to zero to find out the elapsed times at which the altitude

of the rocket is 0. _____

_____

12. You would like the first rocket to detonate when it is at its greatest altitude. For what elapsed time should the fuse be set? Explain how you solved this problem. Do your answers to Exercise 11 help you solve the problem?

_____

_____

_____

Long-Term Project
Fireworks and Quadratic Functions, Chapter 5, page 3

The second rocket will be launched with an initial upward velocity of 144 feet per second.

13. Write a quadratic function to represent the altitude of the second rocket as a function of elapsed time. _____

14. You want the second rocket to burst at an altitude of 320 feet. Use your function to write a quadratic equation by setting $h(t) = 320$. Then rewrite the equation in standard form.

_____

15. Solve the second equation you wrote in Exercise 14 by factoring. For what time should the fuse for this rocket be set? _____

The third and fourth rockets will both be launched with the given initial upward velocities in feet per second and are to burst at the specified altitude in feet.

	Third rocket	Fourth rocket
Initial upward velocity	200	200
Bursting altitude	450	700

16. a. Write a quadratic equation in standard form to represent the altitude of the third rocket when it bursts. _____

b. Write a quadratic equation in standard form to represent the altitude of the fourth rocket when it bursts. _____

17. a. Use the quadratic formula to find the fuse time for the third rocket to the nearest tenth of a second. Explain any unusual results.

_____

b. Use the quadratic formula to find the fuse time for the fourth rocket to the nearest tenth of a second. Explain any unusual results.

_____

You decide to change the bursting altitude of the fourth rocket so that the bursting altitude is at least 580 feet.

18. Write a quadratic inequality to indicate that the bursting altitude must be greater than or equal to 580 feet. Rewrite the inequality so that one side is zero.

_____

19. Write the related quadratic equation by replacing the inequality sign with an equal sign. Give the roots of this equation rounded to the nearest tenth.

_____

Long-Term Project

Fireworks and Quadratic Functions, Chapter 5, page 4

20. On the grid at right, graph the related function for the quadratic equation you solved in Exercise 19. What does the function represent?

_____

_____

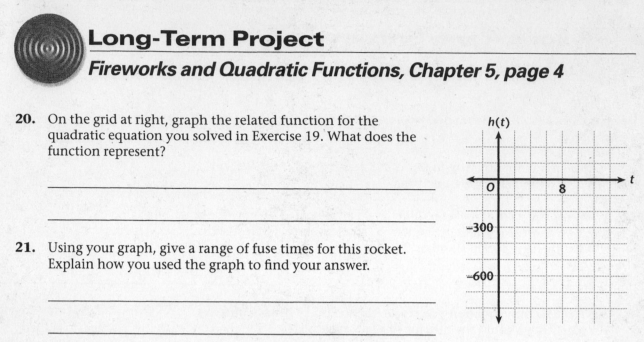

21. Using your graph, give a range of fuse times for this rocket. Explain how you used the graph to find your answer.

_____

_____

_____

_____

Now you must plan the launching and bursting of the next three fireworks in the show. Their initial upward velocities are given in the table below.

Rocket	The Screamer	Mod Quad	Newton's Glory
Velocity (feet per second)	160	200	240

For the safety of the spectators, each rocket must burst at least 350 feet above the ground. At least one rocket should burst at its maximum altitude.

22. Give fuse times for the rockets in the table. Show that you have satisfied the safety requirement by finding the bursting altitude of each rocket. Explain how you found the times and altitudes.

_____

_____

_____

_____

23. Let $h(t) = -16t^2 + v_0t$, where v_0 is positive.

  a. Use the discriminant to show that that there are always two elapsed times at which altitude is 0. _____

  b. Use your answer to part **a** or an analysis of quadratic functions to find the maximum altitude of the rocket. _____

Long-Term Project

Investing, Exponents, and Logarithms, Chapter 6

You have earned $1000 working at a summer job, and you decide to invest that money so that you can buy a computer. The computer that you want costs $1800, and you would like to be able to buy it within 3 years.

Your parents suggest that you go to the local bank and see what types of accounts are available. At the bank, the account representative discusses some options with you. You mention that you will not be withdrawing any money (principal or interest) until the account is worth $1800.

1. The first option is a 1-year Certificate of Deposit (CD) paying 4% interest annually. How much would this account be worth after 3 years?   _____

2. A 3-year Certificate of Deposit pays 5% interest annually. How much would this account be worth after 3 years?   _____

3. The "1-year" and "3-year" periods for these accounts are the lengths of time that you must keep the money in the account. (You pay a penalty if you take the money out before the term is up.) Why might an investor choose a CD with a shorter term rather than a longer one, even though it pays less interest?

   _____

   _____

4. The bank has two other investment opportunities. The first one pays 7% interest each year compounded annually. The second one also pays 7% interest, but the interest is compounded semiannually. Complete each table to see how the initial deposit grows over three years.

   7% interest (annually)

Time	1	2	3
Amount			

   7% interest (semiannually)

Time	0.5	1	1.5	2	2.5	3
Amount						

5. Would any of the four investments above allow you to buy your computer after 3 years? If so, which one(s)?

   _____

Long-Term Project
Investing, Exponents, and Logarithms, Chapter 6, page 2

You are disappointed in these options. A friend's mother is a stockbroker, and she talks to you about the possibility of buying $1000 worth of stock. She tells you that the price of a stock that she has been watching increased by 19% last year. The price of stock in your favorite company declined by 9% last year.

6. Write a function to describe each investment, assuming that these trends continue. Let $A(t)$ represent the amount of the investment after t years.

stock increasing in value 19% per year _____

stock decreasing in value 9% each year _____

7. Using the grid at right, graph the functions you wrote in Exercise 6. Use only positive values of t.

8. Which function represents exponential growth and which function represents exponential decay?

_____

_____

9. Will the investment showing growth be worth $1800 within 3 years? If not, use the graph to approximate how long it will take for the investment to be worth $1800.

Some of your friends suggest that you consider buying collectible items. You go with them to a toy and sports memorabilia show to determine whether this is a good idea.

10. At the show, a basketball-card dealer tells you that a vintage card she bought for $1 increases in value by a factor of 10 every 9 years. If the card is now worth $32, how long ago did she buy it? (Hint: Remember that the value is multiplied by 10 every 9 years, not every year.)

_____

11. Estimate the effective yield of an investment in this basketball card.

_____

12. Would an investment with this annual yield be worth at least $1800 after 3 years?

_____

Long-Term Project

Investing, Exponents, and Logarithms, Chapter 6, page 3

A stuffed animal dealer tells you that a fish he bought for $8 four years ago is now worth $200.

13. Follow the steps below to find the effective yield for this investment.

- Begin with the equation $8(1 + r)^4 = 200$. Solve for $(1 + r)^4$.
- Take the common logarithm of each side of the equation.
- Use the Power Property of Logarithms to rewrite $\log(1 + r)^4$.
- Solve the equation for $\log(1 + r)$.
- Use the Exponential-Logarithmic Inverse Property to eliminate the logarithm. (Hint: Remember that these are common logarithms.) Then solve for r.

_____

14. If current trends continue, how much will a $1000 investment in stuffed fish be worth in 3 years?

_____

15. Under these conditions, how long will it be before you can buy your computer? Explain how you found your answer.

_____

_____

Your parents are worried about some of the investment options you are considering. They ask you to give the bank one more try before making a final decision.

The account representative tells you that they have added an investment account that pays 7% interest compounded continuously.

16. If you invest $1000 in this account, how much will you have after one year? Compare this to the amount you will have if you take the 7% compounded annually and 7% compounded semiannually options.

_____

17. Solve the equation $1000e^{0.07t} = 1800$. Explain what the answer to this equation means.

_____

_____

_____

Long-Term Project

Investing, Exponents, and Logarithms, Chapter 6, page 4

18. Graph $A(t) = 1000e^{0.07t}$ and $A(t) = 1800$ on the grid at right. Use only positive values of t.

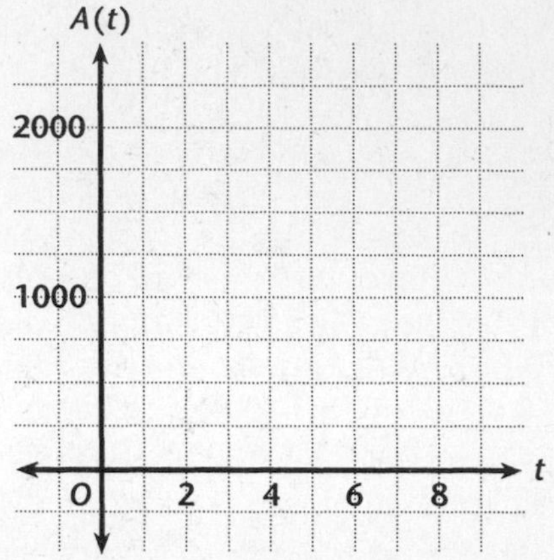

19. Use your graph to check your answer to Exercise 17. Explain how the graph confirms your answer.

_____

_____

_____

_____

It is time to make a decision. You have narrowed your choices down to four options: a Certificate of Deposit (CD), an investment account, a stock, and collectible toys.

20. To help you make your decision, complete the table below.

Investment	Current yield	Risk of losing money	Doubling time	Time to reach $1800	Value after 10 years
CD	4% per year	Very low			
Investment account	7% compounded continuously	Low, although interest rate could change			
Stock	19% per year	Moderate to high			
Collectible toys	5% per *month*	Extremely high			

21. Choose an investment, and explain your decision. (You need not choose an option that earns enough for the computer within 3 years.)

_____

_____

22. If you could distribute the $1000 among more than one of the investments above, would your decision change? Explain your response.

_____

_____

_____

Long-Term Project
Roller Coaster Polynomials, Chapter 7

Fred, Elena, Michael, and Diane enjoy roller coasters. Whenever a new coaster opens near their town, they try to be among the first to ride.

One Saturday, the four friends decide to ride a new coaster. While waiting in line, Fred notices that part of this coaster resembles the graph of a polynomial function that they have been studying in their Algebra 2 class.

1. The brochure for the coaster says that, for the first 10 seconds of the ride, the height of the coaster can be modeled by $h(t) = 0.3t^3 - 5t^2 + 21t$, where t is the time in seconds and h is the height in feet. Classify this polynomial by degree and by number of terms.

   _____

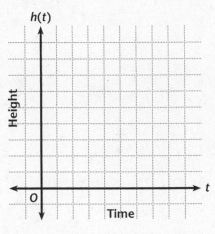

2. Graph the polynomial function for the height of the roller coaster on the grid at right.

3. Use substitution to find the height of the coaster at $t = 0$ seconds. Explain why your answer makes sense.

   _____

4. Find the height of the coaster 9 seconds after the ride begins. _____

5. Evaluate the function for $t = 60$. Why do you think this model is only valid for the first 10 seconds of the ride? (Hint: Mt. Everest is 29,028 feet tall.)

   _____

   _____

Next weekend, Fred, Elena, Michael, and Diane visit another roller coaster. Elena snaps a picture of part of the coaster from the park entrance. The diagram at right represents this part of the coaster.

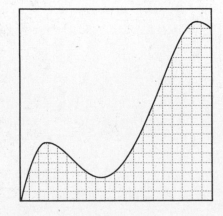

6. Do you think a quadratic, cubic, or quartic function would be the best model for this part of the coaster? Explain your choice.

   _____

   _____

   _____

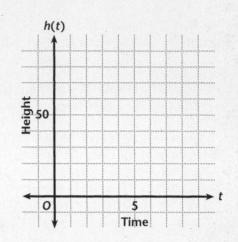

Long-Term Project

Roller Coaster Polynomials, Chapter 7, page 2

7. The part of the coaster captured by Elena on film is modeled by the function below.

    $$h(t) = -0.2t^4 + 4t^3 - 24t^2 + 48t$$

    Graph this polynomial function on the grid at right.

8. Use your graph to approximate the local maxima and minima of this function. Give a real-world interpretation of the maxima and minima.

    _____

    _____

    _____

9. Describe the end behavior of this function.

    _____

10. Suppose that this coaster is a 2-minute ride. Do you think that $h(t) = -0.2t^4 + 4t^3 - 24t^2 + 48t$ is a good model for the height of the coaster throughout the ride? Explain your response.

    _____

    _____

    _____

11. Elena wants to find the height of the coaster when $t = 8$ seconds, 9 seconds, 10 seconds, and 11 seconds. Use synthetic division to find the height of the coaster at this time. Show your work.

    8⌋ -0.2 4 -24 48   0   9⌋ -0.2 4 -24 48   0

    10⌋ -0.2 4 -24 48   0   11⌋ -0.2 4 -24 48   0

Long-Term Project

Roller Coaster Polynomials, Chapter 7, page 3

Michael has studied the history of roller coasters. He believes that the leading cars on roller coasters are becoming more aerodynamic.

12. Michael discovers that the front car of a vintage roller coaster is a rectangular solid whose height is two feet shorter than its width, and whose length is twice its width. The car has a volume of 150 cubic feet.

   a. Write an expression for the car's volume.

   _____

   b. Write an equation showing that the car's volume is equal to 150. Rewrite this equation so that one side is equal to 0.

   _____

   c. Graph the related function for the equation you wrote in part **b**. Use the graph to find the dimensions of the car.

   width: _____

   height: _____

   length: _____

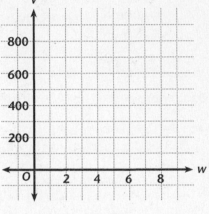

Michael is excited about a proposed coaster in which the cars are made of clear plastic. As shown at right, the first car is shaped like a cylinder with a hemispherical end. The cylindrical part of the car is 8 feet long.

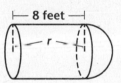

13. Write an expression for the volume of this car.

   _____

14. **a.** The car is to have a volume of 280 cubic feet. Use a graph to find the approximate radius of the car.

   _____

   b. How would the radius of the car change if the volume were changed from 280 cubic feet to 300 cubic feet?

   _____

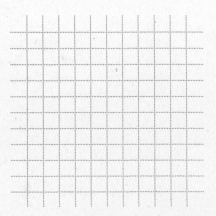

Long-Term Project

Roller Coaster Polynomials, Chapter 7, page 4

Diane's favorite coaster dips into several tunnels during the ride.

15. The 8 seconds of the ride after the coaster comes out of a loop are modeled by $h(t) = -2t^3 + 23t^2 - 59t + 24$.

    a. Graph this polynomial function on the grid at right.

    b. Why do you think the model is only valid from $t = 0$ to $t = 8$?

    _____

    c. Use the graph to estimate the time(s) when the coaster is 50 feet high.

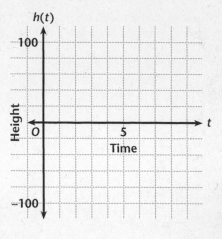

_____

Diane wants to find out when the coaster dips below the ground.

16. **a.** Use the Rational Root Theorem to identify all possible rational zeros of the function $h(t) = -2t^3 + 23t^2 - 59t + 24$.

    _____

    b. Use your graph, synthetic division, and factoring to locate or estimate the real zeros of the function. Interpret the real-world meaning of these zeros.

    _____

    _____

17. Diane is interested in becoming a structural engineer who specializes in roller coaster design. She wants to design a coaster that satisfies the specifications shown at the right.

Help Diane design her coaster by writing a polynomial function that meets these requirements. Show your work.

> • starts at a height of 200 feet
> • dives below the ground at $t = 3$ seconds
> • comes out of the ground at $t = 5$ seconds, then climbs to another peak, and
> • dives beneath the ground again at $t = 10$ seconds.

_____

_____

_____

_____

Long-Term Project

Bicycle Racing and Rational Functions, Chapter 8

Harris High School is holding a bicycle race for charity. The racecourse is shown below. The shortcut E–G–S is an approved part of the course. It allows racers to bypass the route E–F–G–H–S.

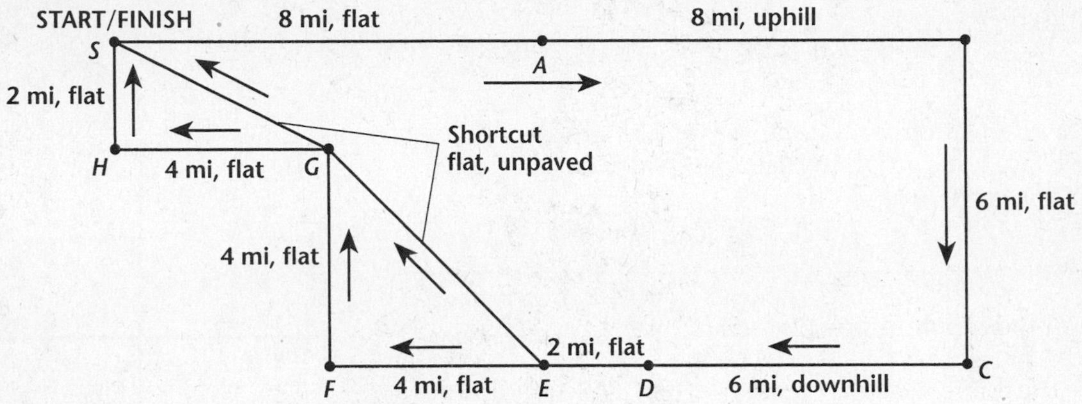

START/FINISH   8 mi, flat   8 mi, uphill

S

2 mi, flat

A

Shortcut
flat, unpaved

6 mi, flat

H   4 mi, flat   G

4 mi, flat

2 mi, flat

F   4 mi, flat   E   D   6 mi, downhill   C

George is just beginning the race. As shown below, his bicycle pedal gear has 52 teeth. During this part of the race, the pedal gear is linked to a rear-wheel gear that has 16 teeth. George's bicycle has 27-inch wheels.

Let t_A and t_B represent the number of teeth on gears A and B, respectively, and let s_A and s_B represent the rotational speeds of the gears A and B, respectively.

If gears A and B have the characteristics shown, then $t_A s_A = t_B s_B$.

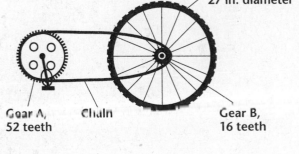

Rear wheel,
27 in. diameter

Gear A,
52 teeth

Chain

Gear B,
16 teeth

1. **a.** Write a combined-variation equation for the rotational speed of gear B. _____

    b. George is turning gear A at 60 revolutions per minute. What is the rotational speed of gear B, in revolutions per minute? _____

    c. Each turn of gear B results in one turn of the bicycle wheel. This moves the bicycle forward a distance equal to the circumference of the rear wheel. Find George's speed in inches per minute. Round your answer to the nearest tenth. _____

    d. Rewrite George's speed in miles per hour. (Hint: First change to inches per hour, then to feet per hour, then to miles per hour.) _____

Long-Term Project

Bicycle Racing and Rational Functions, Chapter 8, page 2

Since $d = rt$, where d represents distance traveled, r represents speed, and t represents elapsed time, the formula $t = \frac{d}{r}$ gives the elapsed time in terms of speed and distance.

The first 8 miles of the race are over flat ground. Fiona rides this portion of the race at r miles per hour.

2. Write an equation for the elapsed time of the first 8 miles of the race in terms of r. What type of variation does this equation represent?

   _____

3. Graph the equation from Exercise 2 on the grid at right.

4. Give the domain of this equation. Then tell what real-world values make sense for r in this situation.

   _____

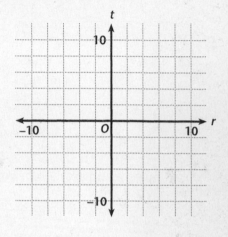

The next 8 miles of the race are uphill, and Fiona's speed decreases to $r - 4$ miles per hour.

5. Write an equation for elapsed time of this portion of the race. Graph this equation on the grid at right.

   _____

6. Give the domain of this equation.

   _____

7. How is this graph related to the one you drew in Exercise 3?

   _____

   _____

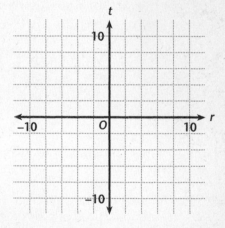

8. If Fiona's speed on flat ground is 15 miles per hour, what is her total time for the first 16 miles of the race, to the nearest hundredth of an hour? Explain how you found your answer.

   _____

   _____

Long-Term Project

Bicycle Racing and Rational Functions, Chapter 8, page 3

Chao and Debbie are the top two finishers in the girls' race. The table below summarizes their performances. Distance is given in miles and speed is given in miles per hour.

	Flat		Uphill		Downhill	
	Distance	Speed	Distance	Speed	Distance	Speed
Chao	30	16.5	8	10	6	20
Debbie	30	s	8	$s-3$	6	18

9. Write an expression for the total time Debbie took to complete the race. Simplify this expression as much as possible. Show your work. _____

10. Debbie took a total of 3 hours to complete the race. Find her speeds for the flat and uphill portions of the race.

_____

_____

11. Find Chao's *average* speed for the race. Is her average speed for the race equal to the average of the three speeds in the table? If not, explain why there is a difference between these averages.

_____

_____

_____

12. Who won the girls' race? By how many minutes did she win? Explain how you solved this problem.

_____

_____

_____

_____

_____

Long-Term Project

Bicycle Racing and Rational Functions, Chapter 8, page 4

Evan and Barry are tied for the lead in the boys' race. They both reach point E at the same time. Evan decides to use the shortcut, E–G–S, an unpaved path, while Barry takes the usual route, E–F–G–H–S, on paved streets.

13. How far does Barry ride from point E to point S?

_____

START/FINISH

14. How long is the shortcut from E to S? Give an exact answer and an answer rounded to the nearest hundredth of a mile.

exact answer: _____

approximation: _____

15. Barry rides to the finish line at b miles per hour. Because of the unpaved path, Evan rides at $20 - b$ miles per hour. For what values of b will Barry win the race? Explain how you solved this problem.

_____

_____

_____

_____

16. Design your own course for a bicycle race. Include different types of terrain that will cause riders to ride at different speeds. Give speeds for an imaginary rider over each type of terrain on your race course. Find the finishing time and average speed for this rider.

terrain: _____

_____

_____

speeds: _____

_____

_____

finishing time /average speed:

_____

Long-Term Project

Conic Sections and Astronomy, Chapter 9

Without the mathematics of conic sections, astronomers could neither explore nor explain our solar system. From the parabolic and hyperbolic reflectors used in radio and optical telescopes to the equations for elliptical orbits, conic sections help us understand and describe the planets.

Although Earth's orbit around the Sun is an ellipse, it is nearly circular. Assume that the Sun is located at (0, 0) and is the center of Earth's orbit.

1. At one point in Earth's orbit, its coordinates, given in millions of miles, are approximately (40, 84). Find the distance between Earth and the Sun.

   _____

2. The equation $x^2 + y^2 = 8649$ models the Earth's orbit. Graph this equation on the grid at right.

3. The moon orbits Earth at an average distance of 0.24 million miles. Write an equation for the moon's orbit when Earth is at (40, 84). (Assume that the moon has a circular orbit, and do not account for the motion of Earth.)

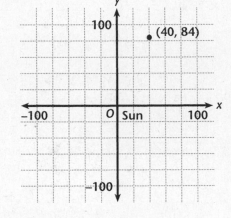

_____

4. Find the areas enclosed by Earth's orbit around the Sun and by the moon's orbit around Earth. About how many times greater is the area enclosed by Earth's orbit?

_____

The orbit of Venus is also nearly circular. The average distance between Venus and the Sun is about 67 million miles.

5. Write an equation for Venus's orbit around the Sun. Then graph the equation on the grid at right.

   _____

In 1962, astronomers used a *radio telescope* at Goldstone, California, to discover that a Venusian day (which begins with the sun rising in the west!) is 243 Earth days long.

Radio telescopes make use of the reflective properties of the parabola. Signals from a distant source are reflected to a common point, the focus of the parabola.

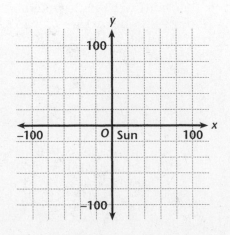

Long-Term Project

Conic Sections and Astronomy, Chapter 9, page 2

6. The National Radio Astronomy Observatory in Green Bank, West Virginia, has a radio telescope whose focus is 60 feet above its vertex.

   a. Write the standard equation of the parabola that is a cross-section of this telescope. Assume that the parabola's vertex is at (0, 0).

   _____

   b. Write an equation for the directrix of the parabola.

   _____

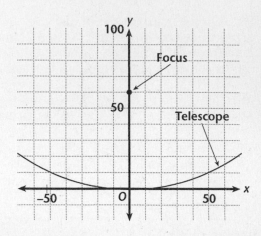

The orbits of all of the planets are actually ellipses with the Sun at one focus. Mercury's orbit is one of the least circular.

7. At its closest approach to the Sun (*perihelion*), Mercury is about 29 million miles from the Sun. At its farthest (*aphelion*), Mercury is about 43 million miles from the Sun.

   a. Graph the aphelion and perihelion of Mercury's orbit on the grid at right. Place the perihelion at (−29, 0). What are the coordinates of the aphelion?

   _____

   b. What is the length of the major axis of this orbit?

   _____

   c. What are the coordinates of the center of the elliptical orbit? Graph this point on the grid. Explain how you found the center.

   _____

   _____

   _____

   d. The minor axis of Mercury's orbit is about 70 million miles long. Write an equation to model Mercury's orbit. Then sketch the orbit on the grid above.

   _____

Long-Term Project

Conic Sections and Astronomy, Chapter 9, page 3

8. Mercury's orbit is one of the *least* circular in the solar system—only Pluto, which was discovered in 1930, has a less circular orbit. Do you think early astronomers would have proposed circular or elliptical orbits for the planets? Explain.

_____

_____

_____

_____

Neptune and Pluto are the solar system's outermost planets. Pluto is usually considered the farthest planet from the Sun—but is this always the case?

9. Neptune's orbit is almost perfectly circular, with a radius of 2.79 *billion* miles. Write an equation to model Neptune's orbit, with the Sun at (0, 0). Then graph Neptune's orbit on the grid at right below.

_____

10. At perihelion, Pluto is about 2.75 billion miles from the Sun. At aphelion, Pluto is about 4.57 billion miles from the Sun.

a. Graph the aphelion and perihelion on the grid at right. Place the perihelion at (−2.75, 0). What are the coordinates of the aphelion?

_____

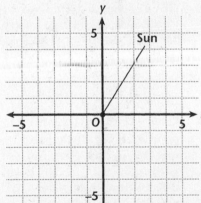

b. What is the length of the major axis of Pluto's orbit? Use your answer to find the coordinates of the center of the orbit. Graph this point on the grid.

_____

c. Using your answers to part **b**, calculate the length of the minor axis of Pluto's orbit.

_____

d. Write an equation to model Pluto's orbit. Then sketch the orbit on the grid above.

_____

Long-Term Project

Conic Sections and Astronomy, Chapter 9, page 4

11. Do the orbits of Neptune and Pluto appear to intersect? If so, how many points of intersection do there appear to be?

_____

12. Consider the equations for the orbits of Neptune and Pluto as a system of nonlinear equations. Solve this system to find the coordinates of any points of intersection of these orbits. Explain how you solved this problem.

_____

_____

13. Is Pluto always the most distant planet from the Sun? Explain.

_____

_____

Asteroids are "minor planets." Thousands of asteroids have been discovered, most orbiting between Mars and Jupiter. However, a few pass closer to the Sun. At perihelion, the asteroid Icarus is 17 million miles from the Sun. At aphelion, it is 183 million miles from the Sun.

14. Give an equation for Icarus's orbit. Graph Icarus's orbit and those of Mercury, Venus, and Earth on the grid at right, with the Sun at (0, 0).

_____

15. Solve a system of equations to find the coordinates of any apparent points of intersection between Icarus's orbit and Earth's orbit. If there are points of intersection, does this mean that Icarus will collide with Earth? (Hint: We are looking at these orbits from "above." Do cars on an overpass collide with those on the road below?)

_____

_____

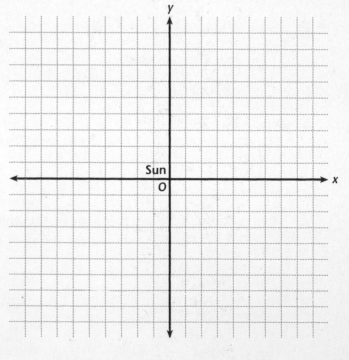

_____

_____

Long-Term Project
Making the Basketball Team, Chapter 10

Michelle, Keiko, Ruth, and Ana are trying out for the Redwood High School varsity girls' basketball team. In all, 21 girls are trying out, and 12 girls will make the team.

The beginning of the first day of tryouts is spent on organizational tasks.

1. The coach wants to divide the players into different groups. At random, each player takes a warm-up jersey from a bin with 9 red, 7 yellow, and 5 blue jerseys. If Ana chooses first, what is the probability that she gets a yellow jersey? Express your answer as a fraction and as a percent rounded to the nearest tenth.

    _____

2. The coach passes around a list of available uniform numbers so that players can indicate their first choices in case they make the team. If the school only has uniforms whose first digits are 1 through 5, inclusive, and whose second digits are 0 through 5, inclusive, how many numbers are on the list?   _____

The coach tells 4 players that they will be trying out for the center position, 8 players that they will be trying out for forward, and 9 players that they will be trying out for guard.

3. The 4 players trying out for center are asked to line up for a rebounding drill. In how many different orders can they line up?   _____

4. The 9 players trying out for guard are asked to form a circle for a passing drill. In how many different orders can they be arranged?   _____

After the first day of tryouts, Keiko, who is the only sophomore trying out, is worried about her chances of making the varsity team.

5. There are 21 players trying out, and 12 will make the team. In how many different ways can the coach choose 12 girls out of 21 players?   _____

6. Although the coach says that no one is guaranteed a spot on the team, 7 of the players trying out this year were on the team last year. If all 7 returning players make the team, in how many ways can the coach select from the other 14 players to complete the team? Explain how you solved this problem.

    _____

    _____

    _____

Long-Term Project

Making the Basketball Team, Chapter 10, page 2

7. Keiko realizes that the different positions people play will affect the decisions the coach makes. Recall that 4 players are trying out for center, 8 for forward, and 9 for guard. If the coach always chooses a team with 2 centers, 5 forwards, and 5 guards, in how many different ways can the team be chosen? Give a detailed explanation of how you solved this problem.

_____

_____

_____

_____

8. Michelle, Keiko, Ruth, and Ana are good friends. They hope that at least two of the four of them make the team. Find the probability that, when 12 girls of the 21 players are chosen, exactly 2 of the 4 friends, chosen at random, make the team. (Assume that every player has an equal chance of

making the team.) _____

After a week of tryouts, the coach posts the list of the players that made the team. The table below summarizes the results.

Class	Made varsity team	Did not make varsity, on JV team	Did not make varsity, decided not to play JV	Total
Sophomore	1	0	0	1
Junior	5	6	1	12
Senior	6	0	2	8
Total	12	6	3	21

9. Did Keiko make the varsity team? How do you know?

_____

_____

10. Find the probability that a randomly-selected player is on the varsity team or the junior varsity (JV) team. _____

11. Find the probability that a randomly-selected player is a junior or is on the varsity team. _____

12. Find the probability that a randomly-selected player is a senior or is on the varsity team. _____

Long-Term Project
Making the Basketball Team, Chapter 10, page 3

Keiko, Michelle, and Ruth made the varsity team. Ruth is a center, Michelle is a forward, and Keiko is a guard.

13. For each pre-season game, the coach selects one team captain at random from the 7 centers and forwards and another at random from the 5 guards. What is the probability that Ruth and Keiko are both selected as captains? _____

14. As part of their pre-season, Redwood plays in a 4-game tournament. What is the probability that a different guard is a team captain in all 4 games?

_____

The coach decides on a starting lineup. The Venn diagram at right indicates the relationship between starting players and returning players.

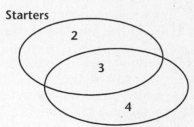

15. What is the probability that a player is a returning player,

given that she is a starter? _____

16. What is the probability that a player is a starter, given that

she is a returning player? _____

Ana did not make the varsity team, but she accepted the coach's offer to become team statistician. Ana analyzed the teams performance in different games. One of her tables is shown below. In the table, the first row indicates how Redwood High School's score compared with that of the opposing team. The second and third rows of the table indicate whether Redwood High School went on to win or lose the game given the halftime status.

Halftime score	10 or more points ahead	1–9 points ahead	Score tied	1–9 points behind	10 or more points behind
Won	6	7	2	3	1
Lost	1	2	1	2	2

17. If Redwood High School was ahead at halftime of a particular game, what is the probability that the team won that game? Explain how you solved this problem.

_____

_____

18. If Redwood High School was behind or tied at halftime, what is the probability that the team won the game? Explain how you solved this problem.

_____

Long-Term Project

Making the Basketball Team, Chapter 10, page 4

Redwood High School has made the regional tournament for the northern half of the state! This year, the tournament is a double-elimination format. To advance to the state finals, a team must win 4 games without losing 2 of them.

Coin tosses	Result of tournament (won/lost)

19. Suppose that Redwood's probability of winning any single game is 50%. Use a simulation to estimate the probability that Redwood advances to the state finals.
    - Use a coin toss to simulate each game. Let heads represent a win and tails a loss.
    - A trial ends when Redwood has won 4 games or lost 2 games, whichever comes first.
    - Run 10 trials. Record the results of each in the table at right.
    - Give the probability that Redwood wins the regional tournament.

    _____

20. Based on your simulation, how many games should Redwood High School expect to play in the tournament?

    _____

Redwood High beats the odds, and their team goes to the state championship game! Unfortunately, Redwood falls behind, and the coach calls time out with 3 minutes left. The team is trailing by 7 points. The coach estimates that Redwood will have the ball only 8 more times.

Throughout the season, Ana recorded the points scored by Redwood each time they had the ball. These statistics are shown below.

Outcome	0 points	1 point	2 points
Probability	$\frac{3}{6}$	$\frac{1}{6}$	$\frac{2}{6}$

21. Assume that Redwood holds the opposing team scoreless over the last 3 minutes.

    - Use a simulation with 10 trials to estimate the probability that Redwood ties or wins the game by scoring 7 or more points the next 8 times they have the ball.

    - On a separate sheet of paper, explain how you conducted your simulation, give a table showing the results, and give your estimate of the probability that Redwood will win or tie the game.

NAME _____ CLASS _____ DATE _____

Long-Term Project
Designing a Theater, Chapter 11

The city council has decided to fund a small theater for community plays. You have been selected student representative to the committee that is evaluating different theater design proposals.

An architectural firm proposes three options. Option A has the seating plan shown below. The first three rows are shown.

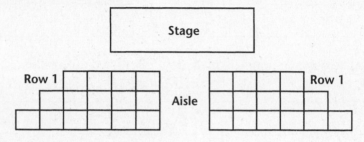

1. Write the first three terms of the sequence that describes the number of seats in each row. _____

2. Write an explicit formula for the number of seats in the nth row of the theater in option A. _____

3. Write a recursive formula for the number of seats in the nth row of the theater. _____

4. a. Use either the explicit or the recursive formula to find the number of seats in the 8th row of the theater. _____

    b. Which formula did you use to solve this problem? Explain why you used this formula.

    _____

    _____

5. Option A has 9 rows of seats. Find the average number of seats in each row by finding the arithmetic mean of the number of seats in row 1 and the number of seats in row 9. _____

6. The blueprint for option B shows that the number of seats in each row is given by $t_n = 4n + 4$. Find the number of seats in the first 5 rows for this design. _____

7. Option B has 7 rows of seats. Find the average number of seats in each row by finding the arithmetic mean of the number of seats in row 1 and the number of seats in row 7. _____

Long-Term Project
Designing a Theater, Chapter 11, page 2

Under either Option A or B, the theater must seat at least 125 people.

8. Evaluate $\sum_{n=1}^{7}(4n+4)$. What does this sum represent in this real-world situation?

   _____

   _____

9. Find the seating capacity for Option A. Explain how you solved this problem.

   _____

   _____

10. Which option seats more people, Option A or Option B? In which design are seats farther from the stage? Choose one of these options and explain why you prefer this option.

    _____

    _____

    _____

In Option C, there are seats on two sides of the stage. This design has the seating plan shown at right. In this design, a row refers to a set of seats in line and the corresponding seats on the other side of the stage.

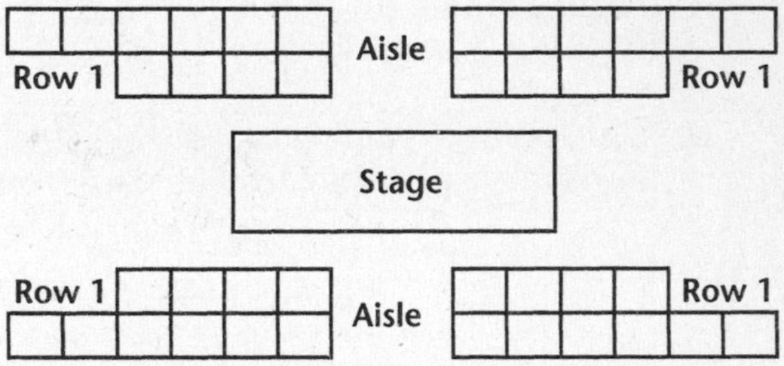

11. Row 1 of this design has 16 seats. How many seats are in Row 2?

    _____

12. Find the ratio of the number of seats in Row 1 to Row 2. _____

13. The seating pattern in this option can be described by a *geometric* sequence. Write an explicit formula for the number of seats in the *n*th row. Explain why the sequence is geometric and how you found the formula.

    _____

    _____

Long-Term Project

Designing a Theater, Chapter 11, page 3

14. There are four rows of seats in this design.
Find the number of seats in Row 4. _____

15. Can the seats in Row 4 be arranged symmetrically, that is, with the same number of seats on each side of the stage, and the same number of seats on the right and left side of each aisle? If so, explain how. If not, tell how you would arrange the seats in this row.

_____

_____

16. Find $\sum\limits_{n=1}^{4} t_n$, where t_n is the explicit formula you wrote in Exercise 13.

Does this theater design seat at least 125 people?

_____

_____

17. You must make a recommendation to the committee supporting one of these options. Write a brief report explaining the advantages and disadvantages of each design. Which design seems the best? Explain.

_____

_____

_____

_____

_____

Jasmine feels that ticket prices for the theater should be based on row number, so that people in Row 1 pay the highest prices, those in Row 2 the next highest, and so on. She proposes a geometric sequence for the prices.

18. She recommends that Row 1 tickets cost $12.50 and Row 5 tickets cost $5.12. Find the three positive geometric means between these prices. What do the geometric means represent in this context?

_____

_____

_____

Long-Term Project
Designing a Theater, Chapter 11, page 4

The city council thinks that people who attend plays at the local junior college will also be interested in going to the community theater. They ask you to have volunteers set up an information booth at one of the junior college theaters. The volunteers pass out ticket forms for the community theater to interested patrons.

19. You estimate that about half of the people who take the ticket forms will eventually buy tickets.

    a. Find the probability that, in a group of 6 people who take the ticket forms, at least 4 will buy tickets to the community theater production   _____

    b. Explain how you solved this problem.

    _____

    _____

    _____

20. Use a calculator to find the probability that, if 50 people take the ticket forms, 23, 24, 25, or 26 of them will buy tickets.

_____

The city council is not entirely happy with any of the theater plans that have been submitted. They ask you to explore other ideas.

21. On a separate sheet of paper, develop a plan for your own community theater to present at the next city council meeting. Your plan should include each of the following:

    • a sketch of a seating plan in which the number of seats in each row follows an arithmetic or geometric sequence. The plan should include at least 125 seats.

    • the total seating capacity of the theater

    • a ticket pricing plan in which the price of tickets in each row follows an arithmetic or geometric sequence

Long-Term Project
Movie Statistics, Chapter 12

A large movie theater chain, hearing of your statistical expertise, hires you to assist its marketing department in a study of its theaters. Your first task is to analyze the statistics for current hit movies. The data in the table below shows the weekly earnings for the top ten movies in a certain week. It also gives the number of screens on which each movie was shown.

1. Complete the last row of the table.

Rank	1	2	3	4	5	6	7	8	9	10
Weekly earnings (in thousands of dollars)	36,400	26,300	20,800	14,100	11,900	11,400	10,200	9800	7500	6200
Number of screens	2601	2719	2610	2095	2411	2057	2447	2447	2098	2330
Weekly earnings per screen (in thousands of dollars)										

2. Find the mean and median of the weekly box office receipts for the top ten movies. Explain why this data set has no mode.

mean: _____   median: _____

_____

_____

3. Find the mean and median earnings per screen for the top ten movies.

mean: _____   median: _____

4. The manager of one of the theaters is certain that she will be able to run a top-ten movie every week. She wants your best estimate for the typical weekly earnings of a top-ten movie. What would you tell her? Explain.

_____

_____

5. Suppose that in the next week, the number-one movie earned twice as much money—$72,800,000—while the other movies earned the same amounts. Calculate its weekly earnings per screen and the new mean and median earnings per screen for the top ten movies. Would you change the estimate you gave to the manager? Why or why not?

earnings: _____   mean: _____   median: _____

_____

Long-Term Project
Movie Statistics, Chapter 12, page 2

The marketing department wants to know whether most movie attendance comes from a few people who attend movies regularly or from a large number of people who only attend occasionally.

6. You ask 20 moviegoers to estimate the number of times they go to the movies each month. Their responses are given below.

    1   3   2 10 21   4 15   6   2   1
    7 14 12   5   4 20   2 10   6   1

Make a stem-and-leaf plot of this data.

Stem	Leaf

7. What is the total number of movie tickets purchased by these people in a typical month? How many of these tickets were purchased by the 5 most frequent moviegoers?

_____

8. Would you suggest that the marketing department advertise in movie magazines, which are read by frequent moviegoers, or billboards, which are seen by a wide range of people? Justify your answer.

_____

_____

A large part of the theater's revenues comes from concession stands, where people buy food and drinks. However, the company has never done a detailed analysis of the purchases at these stands. The head of the marketing department asks you to do a preliminary investigation.

9. To begin your investigation, you find the amounts spent by 40 customers at the concession stand. To the nearest dollar, these amounts are:

   9   8   5   3   8   4 11   2   4   1   4   7   8   6
  12   7   3   8   6   7   5   8   9   5   7 10   2   9
   7   4   7   4   3   6   8 10   2   8   6   7

Organize this data in the frequency table below.

Amount spent	1	2	3	4	5	6	7	8	9	10	11	12
Frequency												

10. Make a histogram of the spending at this concession stand using the frequency table.

11. Find the quartiles, range, and interquartile range for this data set. Are there any outliers?

_____

_____

Long-Term Project
Movie Statistics, Chapter 12, page 3

12. The data listed in Exercise 9 was collected at noon on a Saturday. You decide to collect data for another day of the week and time of day. The receipts for Tuesday night at 9:00 P.M., arranged in numerical order, are:

```
1  1  2  2  2  2  2  3  3  3  3   4  4  4
4  4  4  4  4  5  5  5  5  5  5   5  6  6
6  6  6  6  7  7  7  7  8  8  9  12
```

Find the quartiles, range, and interquartile range for this data set. Are there any outliers?

_____

13. Sketch box-and-whisker plots at right for the data sets listed in Exercises 9 and 12.

14. Compare these box-and-whisker plots. How does concession spending differ for these times? What might some reasons for the differences be?

_____

_____

_____

```
<--+--+--+--+--+--+--+--+--+--+--+--+-->
   0  1  2  3  4  5  6  7  8  9 10 11 12
            Amount spent
```

15. Use a calculator to find the standard deviation for the two data sets. Describe what the standard deviations indicate about the data sets.

_____

_____

The marketing department is considering a "See It Again, Sam" promotion to encourage customers to see the same top-ten movie more than once. They would like to have a 50% probability that at least 2 out of 5 customers see the movie again.

16. The marketing department estimates that, under normal circumstances, 12% of customers will see a top-ten movie again. Find the probability that, in a group of 5 viewers of a particular movie, at least 2 will see the movie again. _____

17. The "See It Again, Sam" promotion gives customers a $2 coupon for a repeat viewing of a movie. The marketing department hopes that, with this coupon, 20% of viewers will see the movie again. Under these circumstances, what is the probability at least 2 out of 5 viewers return? _____

Long-Term Project

Movie Statistics, Chapter 12, page 4

The marketing department is not encouraged by your answer to Exercise 17.
They ask you to investigate the effect of changing the discount from $2 to $4.

18. Estimate the percent of moviegoers that you think will see a top-ten
movie again with a $4 discount. (Choose a percent greater than 20% but
less than 100%.) Find the probability that at least 2 out of 5 viewers
return if they are given a $4 discount.

_____

19. Based on your answer to Exercise 18, should the marketing department
offer the $4 discount? (Recall that the department would like a 50%
probability that at least 2 out of 5 customers return.)

_____

Your help on earlier projects has convinced the theater of the value of
statistical research. The company decides to conduct a large-scale study of
attendance at one of its 8-screen theaters.

20. In analyzing the attendance data, you find that the number of tickets
sold at the theater on a given day is approximately normally distributed,
with a mean of 2500 tickets and a standard deviation of 700 tickets. Find
the probability that, on a given day, the number of tickets sold at this
theater is between 1800 and 3200.   _____

21. What is the probability that the theater sells between 2000 and 2800
tickets on a given day?   _____

22. This theater loses money if fewer than 1900 tickets are sold. What is the
probability that the theater loses money on a particular day?   _____

As a reward for your good work, the marketing department gives you funds for
a study of your own.

23. Gather real numerical data about moviegoing habits or preferences by
surveying people at your school, or by collecting data from newspapers,
magazines, and internet sources. On a separate sheet of paper, prepare a
report on your findings. Your report should include:

- your data and an explanation of how it was gathered,

- the mean, median, mode (if any), and standard deviation of your data
set, and

- at least 2 of the following: a stem-and-leaf plot, a box-and-whisker
plot, a circle graph, and a histogram.

Long-Term Project
A Sinusoidal Shipwreck, Chapter 13

Captain Green of the salvage ship *Doubloon* has invited you to go on a search for the wreck of the 16th century galleon *Piarsquare*. You will use trigonometry to find the wreck, evade your competitors, pick up the treasure, and return home safely.

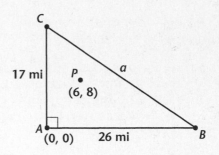

1. The *Piarsquare* sank somewhere in the region bounded by the triangle shown at right. Solve for m∠C, m∠B, and *a*. Round your answers to the nearest tenth.

_____

2. You are currently at point *A*, coordinates (0, 0), and are headed directly toward point *B*. The captain decides that the most likely location for the wreck of the *Piarsquare* is *P*(6, 8). Through what angle should the salvage ship turn to head for point *P*? Explain how you solved this problem.

_____

_____

The *Doubloon* is not the only ship searching for the *Piarsquare!* Captain O'Mean is attempting to follow your ship to the treasure and claim it for himself. The radar operator on the *Doubloon* keeps watch for Captain O'Mean's ship on the radar screen shown at right.

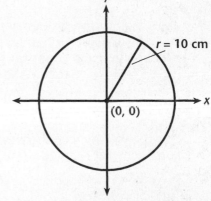

3. As you watch, the line on the radar screen rotates. It begins in standard position and rotates through 840°. Find an angle coterminal to the 840° angle. The measure of the coterminal angle should be between 0° and 360°.

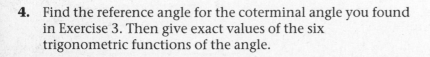

4. Find the reference angle for the coterminal angle you found in Exercise 3. Then give exact values of the six trigonometric functions of the angle.

_____

5. The line on the screen makes one revolution in 2 minutes. Find the angular speed of the tip of the arm in radians per second. Then convert this speed to degrees per second.

_____

Long-Term Project

A Sinusoidal Shipwreck, Chapter 13, page 2

6. Find the linear speed of the point at the tip of the rotating line.
Give your answer is centimeters per second.

_____

7. A blip appears at the very tip of the radar arm when it is at an angle of
248°, the angle being in standard position. You suspect it is Captain
O'Mean's ship. If the center of the radar screen is at (0, 0), and the radius
of the radar screen is 10 centimeters, what are the coordinates of the blip
on the screen?

_____

8. You need to take evasive action. The *Doubloon* is at (0, 0) and is headed
along the positive *x*-axis. You want to turn so your ship's path is heading
away from Captain O'Mean's current position as quickly as possible.
Through what angle should you turn? Explain.

_____

_____

_____

The *Doubloon*'s echolocation system is scanning the sea floor for traces of the
Piarsquare. Finally, some traces that could be a ship's outline appear.

9. The echolocation system locates the shipwreck at
an angle of depression of 12° and a distance of
2200 meters from your ship. At what depth *d*
would you expect to find the wreck?

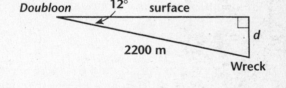

_____

10. Due to a nearby reef, the wreck is most safely
approached at high tide. Over the next 24 hours,
the tides can be modeled by $h = 1.6 \sin \frac{\pi}{6}(t - 4)$,
where *h* is the height above sea level in meters and
t is the number of hours since midnight.

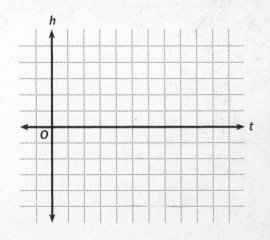

   a. Identify the amplitude, period, phase shift, and
   vertical translation of this function.

   _____

   _____

   b. Graph this function on the grid at right. Be sure
   to show times from *t* = 0 hours to 24 hours.

Long-Term Project

A Sinusoidal Shipwreck, Chapter 13, page 3

11. Use your graph from Exercise 10 to find the safest time(s) to approach the wreck. Express your answers as times of day, given that midnight is at $t = 0$.

_____

12. What times are the *least* safe for approaching the wreck?

_____

The *Doubloon* sails over the reef safely and anchors itself directly over the wreck. Due to shark-infested waters, diving is unsafe, so a robotic probe is sent to explore the wreck and recover its treasures.

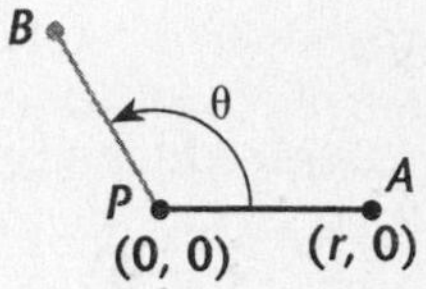

A simplified version of the probe's robotic arm is shown at right. The arm pivots at point P, and can be returned to its normal position $\overline{PA}$ by pressing a reset button. The arm, $\overline{BP}$, can also be lengthened or shortened as desired.

13. The robot's video camera shows a jeweled goblet at $(-9, 10)$. The robotic arm's operator sets the length of the arm to $r = 30$ centimeters and turns it counterclockwise 138°.

a. What are the coordinates of B after the turn? Explain.

_____

_____

b. Is B on the goblet?

_____

c. Did the arm operator turn the arm through the correct angle θ? If not, what is the correct angle? Explain how to find the correct angle.

_____

_____

d. Did the operator set the correct arm length r? If not, what is the correct length? Explain.

_____

_____

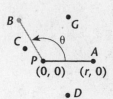

Long-Term Project
A Sinusoidal Shipwreck, Chapter 13, page 4

As shown at right, there are three more priceless treasures to be picked up by the robot arm:

- a gold medallion G at (18.9, 27)

- a rare coin C at (−12, 8), and

- a diamond necklace D at (15.8, −17.3)

You can turn the arm counterclockwise any number of degrees and change its length.

14. Find values of r and θ that will move point B to the treasures at G, C, and D. Round measures to the nearest tenth.

    a. G _____

    b. C _____

    c. D _____

Now that you have recovered the treasures, it is time to head for the harbor, which is located at point T. The ship must follow the route from P to Q to R to S to T shown below. All distances are in nautical miles.

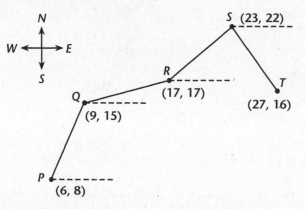

15. Plan the route for the return trip. Describe each segment of the route by giving its length and the angle the segment should make with due east.

_____

_____

_____

_____

_____

Long-Term Project
A Ski Vacation, Chapter 14

Seven friends are planning a ski weekend. Four of them, María, Alan, David, and Joyce, enjoy cross-country skiing. The others, Jerome, Patrick, and Sarah, prefer downhill skiing.

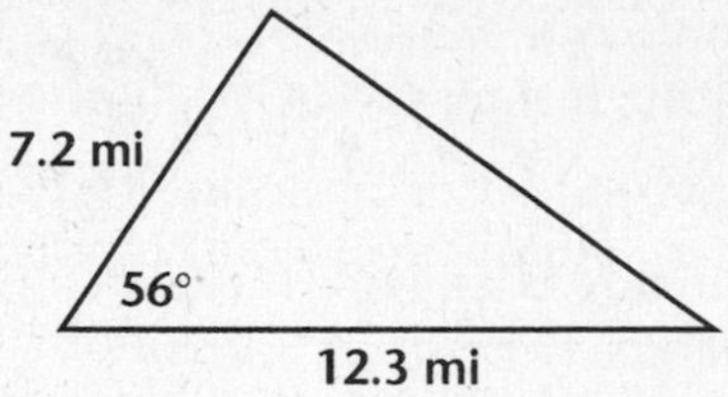

1. The part of the ski resort that is reserved for cross-country skiing is shown at right. What is the area of this region?

    _____

2. The ski resort is on a mountain. When the friends are 4 kilometers away from the base of the mountain, the angle of elevation to its peak is 8°. When they arrive at the base of the mountain, the angle of elevation to the peak is 35°

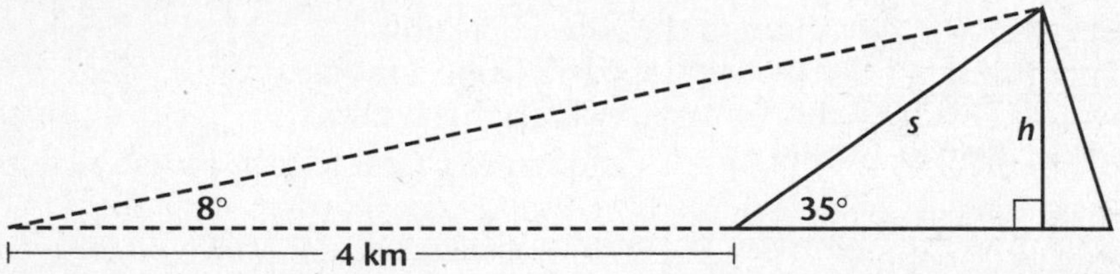

    a. Use the law of sines to find s, the length of a side of the mountain. Round your answer to the nearest thousandth of a kilometer, then convert your answer to meters.

    _____

    b. Find the height, h, of the mountain to the nearest meter. Explain how you solved this problem.

    _____

    _____

As Alan and Joyce leave the ski lodge, they see a notice indicating that the cross-country trail from A to B is under repair. They must take the detour through C shown at right.

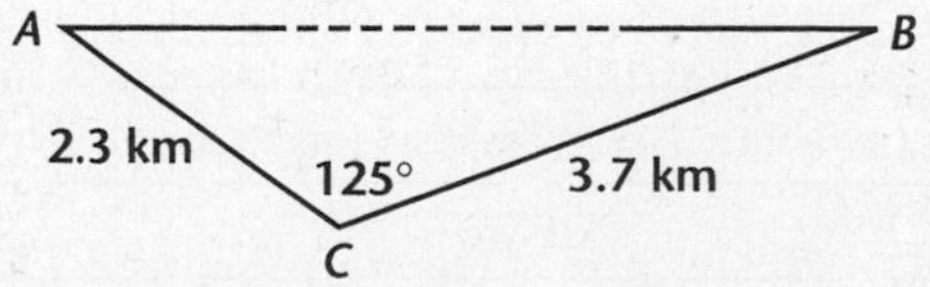

3. How much longer is the detour than the direct path? Round your answer to the nearest tenth of a kilometer. Which trigonometric law did you use to solve this problem?

    _____

    _____

Long-Term Project

A Ski Vacation, Chapter 14, page 2

María and David are part of a volunteer ski patrol. A skier has been reported missing, so they leave patrol headquarters H to begin a search.

4. As shown, María and David go in different directions. María, skiing on a difficult trail, skis at 4.4 kilometers per hour. David skis at 4.8 kilometers per hour. After $1\frac{1}{2}$ hours, María radios David that she has found the missing skier. How far apart are María and David when she locates the skier?

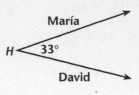

_____

5. How long will it take David to reach María if he skis to her at a speed of 4.8 kilometers per hour?   _____

6. Skiers wax their skis to move more easily through the snow. If a snow-covered slope is steep enough, a ski placed on the slope will begin to slide by itself. The minimum angle θ with the horizontal at which this occurs can be found by solving the equation below.

   $\sin \theta = \mu_s \cos \theta$, where μ_s is the coefficient of static friction

   a. A skier uses a wax with a μ_s value of 0.12. Find the angle at which a ski begins to slide with this wax. Round your answer to the nearest tenth of a degree.   _____

   b. A skier uses a wax with a μ_s value of 0.15. Find the angle at which the ski begins to slide.   _____

   c. Which coefficient of friction, 0.12 or 0.15, represents a "slipperier" wax? Explain.

   _____

   _____

Jerome, Patrick, and Sarah buy their lift tickets and go to the line for the gondola, which begins partway up the mountain.

7. The length of the gondola ride, length of the ski run, and distance from the bottom of the run to the gondola are shown in the diagram at right. Find m$\angle A$, the incline of the ski lift, and m$\angle DBC$, the incline of the side of the mountain.

   _____

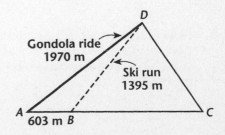

Long-Term Project

A Ski Vacation, Chapter 14, page 3

8. At the top of the ski lift, the chairs are rotated so that they face the opposite direction for the return trip down the mountain. Chair A is at (12, 0) as it begins the rotation.

a. Find the rotation matrix R_{60} for a 60° rotation.

$$R_{60} = \begin{bmatrix} & \\ & \end{bmatrix}$$

b. Find the coordinates of the image of chair A after a 60° rotation. Round coordinates to the nearest tenth.

_____

c. The chair must rotate another 120° to reverse its direction. Find the rotation matrix for a 120° rotation.

$$R_{120} = \begin{bmatrix} & \\ & \end{bmatrix}$$

d. Use the coordinates you found in part **b** to find the final position of chair A. Explain why your answer makes sense.

_____

_____

After his first ski run, Jerome looks up the mountain to watch for Sarah and Patrick. He notices that skiers' paths look like sine waves as they move down the mountain, as shown at right.

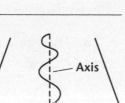

9. Suppose that a skier's path can be modeled by $s(t) = 10 \sin \pi t$, where t is the time in seconds and s is the distance, in meters, to the left (negative) or right (positive) of the axis of the path.

a. Graph $s(t)$ on the grid at right. Include t-values from 0 to 2 seconds. (Hint: Be sure to use radians.)

b. Write an equation showing that skier is 8 meters to the right of the axis of his or her path.

_____

c. For what t-values between 0 seconds and 2 seconds is the skier 8 meters to the right of the axis of the path? Round your answer to the nearest tenth.

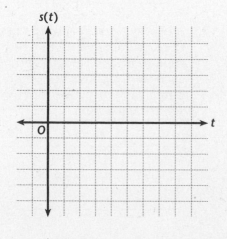

Long-Term Project

A Ski Vacation, Chapter 14, page 4

A ski jumping competition is being held at a nearby mountain. The friends decide to spend part of their afternoon watching the competition.

10. For a particular jump, the horizontal and vertical distances covered by the skier in t seconds are given by $x(t) = 25t \cos \theta$ and $y(t) = 25t \sin \theta - 4.9t^2$. Distances $x(t)$ and $y(t)$ are measured in meters.

    a. At what angle did the jumper take off if he lands at the base of a 90-meter hill after 5.1 seconds? (Hint: Let $y(5.1) = -90$.)

    _____

    b. How much horizontal distance did the jump cover?

    _____

11. The snow depth at the top of the mountain is reported in the local newspaper. For the past few months, Patrick has been recording this data. By running a sinusoidal regression on his graphics calculator, he finds that the depth of the snow is modeled by $d(t) = 45 \cos \frac{2\pi}{365}t + 40$, where t is given in days, and $t = 0$ on January 1. The snow depth d is given in inches.

    a. The resort is only open when the snow depth exceeds 60 inches. Between what dates would you expect the resort to be closed?

    _____

    b. When is there no snow on the mountain? Explain.

    _____

    _____

12. A nearby resort is adding a new gondola to the top of its mountain. Use the diagram at right to find the length of the lift. Show each step in your solution process, and name any laws or identities you used to solve the problem.

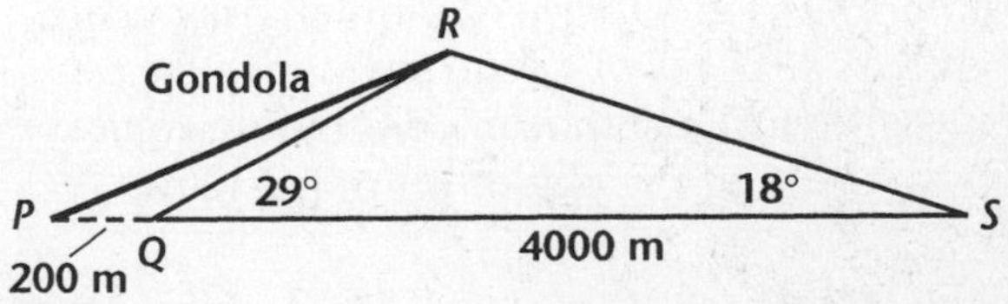

    _____

    _____

    _____

ANSWERS

Long-Term Project — Chapter 1

1. Answers may vary. Sample answers: smallest; 8700; largest: 8940; vertical axis increment: 15

2.
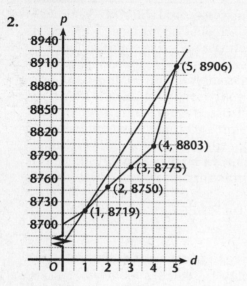

3. increasing at a steady rate until Day 5, when it jumps dramatically

4. **a.** See graph above.
   b. $\frac{187}{4}$
   c. Over 4 days, the stocks increased 187 points.
   d. $p = 46.75d + 8672.25$

5. **a.** 9139.75
   b. 9373.5
   c. 9607.25
   d. 9841

6. Answers may vary. Sample answer: No; the stock market varies too much to be modeled by a linear function, especially one determined by a very small set of data.

7. $p \approx 42.7d + 8662.5$

8. **a.** 9089.5
   b. 9303
   c. 9516.5
   d. 9730

9. Answers may vary. Sample answer: The values obtained from the equation in Exercise 8 are lower than those found in Exercise 5.

10. Answers may vary. Sample answer: No; the model is based on data from a record-breaking week.

11. **a.** 0.94
    b. Answers may vary. Sample answer: A high correlation coefficient tells you that the equation models the data well, but that data may not be representative of long-term trends.

12. Answers may vary. Sample answer: The data is not a good sample, because the stock market goes up and down but this data has a completely upward trend.

13. -0.5

14. Answers may vary. Sample answer: No; the Nasdaq data goes up and down.

15. **a.** $p \approx -0.6d + 41.8$
    b. -0.249
    c. Answers may vary. Sample answer: The equation does show a downward trend shown by the negative slope, but the correlation coefficient shows that the correlation is not reliable. It is not close to -1.

16. **a.** 35.8
    b. 32.8
    c. 29.8
    d. 26.8

17. Answers may vary. Sample answer: The Nasdaq and Dow Indices do not show the same trends.

18. Answers may vary. Sample answer: According to Dow Jones, stocks will go up about 7%, but according to Nasdaq, stocks will go down about 12%.

19. **a.** Answers may vary. Sample answer: The Nasdaq is a more conservative indicator of future trends on the stock market than the Dow Jones index.
    b. Answers may vary. Sample answer: The Dow Jones data may be overly optimistic even though the correlation coefficient was more reliable.

ANSWERS

20. a. Close, Change

b. Answers may vary. Sample answers: Let x represent percent change. Let C represent closing price and G represent change. Then $x = \dfrac{100G}{C - G}$.

21.

Index	Percent change
30 Industrials	-0.86
20 Transports	-2.01
15 Utilities	-0.68
65 Stocks	-1.17

22. Answers may vary. Sample answer: All the indices went down, but the Utilities went down the least, so utilities might be a less risky investment.

23. Low < Close < High

24. Answers may vary. Two samples are given.

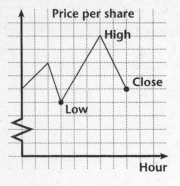

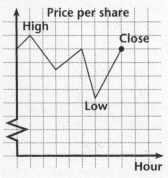

Long-Term Project — Chapter 2

1. a.

r	1	2	3	4	5	6	7
f_c	0.44	0.88	1.32	1.75	2.19	2.63	3.07

b. f_c varies directly with r. The constant of variation is $\dfrac{4\pi^2(2.5)}{15^2}$, or ≈ 0.44.

2. a.

m	1	2	3	4	5	6	7
f_c	0.23	0.47	0.70	0.94	1.17	1.41	1.64

b. f_c varies directly with m. The constant of variation $\dfrac{4\pi^2(18)}{55^2}$, or ≈ 0.23.

3. For each value of m, r, and T, there is exactly one value of f_c. Each variable must represent a positive quantity.

4. Both objects will complete one orbit in the same time because $\sqrt{\dfrac{4\pi^2(10)(3)}{f_c}} = \sqrt{\dfrac{4\pi^2(3)(10)}{f_c}}$ by the Commutative Property of Multiplication.

5. $T = \sqrt{\left(\dfrac{t^2R^2}{r^2}\right)\left(\dfrac{R}{r}\right)} = \left(\left(\dfrac{t^2R^2}{r^2}\right)\left(\dfrac{R}{r}\right)\right)^{0.5} = \left(\dfrac{t^2R^2}{r^2}\right)^{0.5}\left(\dfrac{R}{r}\right)^{0.5} = \dfrac{tR}{r}\left(\dfrac{R}{r}\right)^{0.5} = \dfrac{tR}{r}\sqrt{\dfrac{R}{r}}$

6. 0.61; the Venus year is about 61% as long as an Earth year.

7. 1.89; the Martian year is about 1.89 Earth years.

8. a. 1.12×10^{-12}; $T = 1.12 \times 10^{-12}\, R\sqrt{R}$

ANSWERS

b.

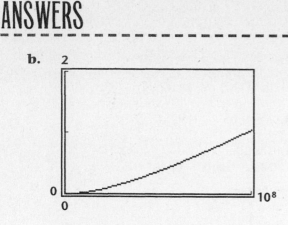

c. As R increases, T increases. However, the graph is more complex than a direct variation graph.

9. about 121,864,475 miles

10. Yes; the graph shows that the given function passes the horizontal-line test. So the function has an inverse function that gives R for a given value of T.

11. $V_c = \dfrac{\pi r^2 h}{3}$

12. $V_s = \pi r^2 H$

13. $V_h = \dfrac{2\pi r^3}{3}$

14. $V_f = V_c + V_s + V_h = \dfrac{\pi r^2 h}{3} + \pi r^2 H + \dfrac{2\pi r^3}{3}$

15. 1479.65 cubic meters

16. $V_f = \dfrac{19\pi r^2 h}{3} + \dfrac{2\pi r^3}{3}$

17. $V_f = \dfrac{21.5\pi r^3}{3}$

18. V_f is a function of h, H, and r, and h and H are functions of r, so V_f is a composite function.

19. a. $V_f - V_i = \dfrac{4\pi r^3}{3}$

b. The difference in volumes is twice the amount that protrudes, $\dfrac{2\pi r^3}{3}$.

c. 310.34 cubic meters

20. a. The length of the nested set of columns is $L + (n-1)s$. The total length may not exceed 20. Thus, $L + (n-1)s \le 20$.

b. $L + (n-1)s \le 20$; $(n-1)s \le 20 - L$; $n - 1 \le \dfrac{20 - L}{s}$; $n \le \dfrac{20 - L}{s} + 1$.
Since n is a positive integer, take $\left[\dfrac{20 - L}{s} + 1\right]$.

21. a. $n = [201 - 10L]$

b.

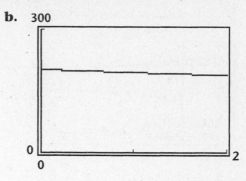

The graph involves a reflection across the y-axis, followed by a horizontal compression by a factor of $\dfrac{1}{10}$, followed by a horizontal translation 201 units to the left.

22. $s = \dfrac{tL}{r_2 - r_1} = \left(\dfrac{t}{r_2 - r_1}\right)L$; if t, r_1, and r_2 are held constant, then $\dfrac{t}{r_2 - r_1}$ is also constant. So the function is a direct-variation relationship with constant of variation $\dfrac{t}{r_2 - r_1}$.

23. 20

Long-Term Project — Chapter 3

1. a. Females: $19.85x + 33.74y = 1500$
Males: $19.85x + 33.74y = 1200$

b. Females: $4.51x + 0.03y = 12$
Males: $4.51x + 0.03y = 12$

2. Female:

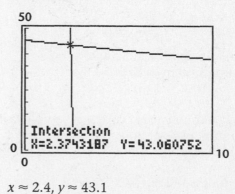

$x \approx 2.4$, $y \approx 43.1$

ANSWERS

Male:

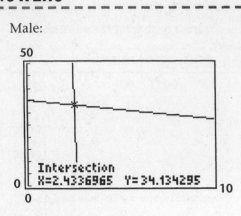

$x \approx 2.4$ and $y \approx 34.1$

3. a. Females: 43.1 ounces, about 5.4 cups, of milk, 2.4 ounces of cereal
Males: 34.1 ounces, about 4.3 cups of milk, 2.4 ounces of cereal

b. Answers may vary. Sample answer: The serving of milk would be better spread out over a day. The cereal is a reasonable amount for breakfast.

4. Females:
$$\begin{cases} 4.51x + 0.03y = 3.6 \\ 19.85x + 33.74y = 450 \end{cases}$$
$x \approx 0.7$, $y \approx 12.9$
Males:
$$\begin{cases} 4.51x + 0.03y = 3.6 \\ 19.85x + 33.74y = 360 \end{cases}$$
$x \approx 0.7$, $y \approx 10.2$
No; the serving of milk is about one glass, but it is likely that one would eat more cereal than this amount.

5. Answers may vary. Sample answers: (using requirements for male, and steak and swiss cheese for the food items.) Let x represent the number of ounces of steak, and y represent the number of ounces of cheese.
$$\begin{cases} 0.85x + 0.06y = 6 \\ 1.98x + 272.44y = 600 \end{cases}$$

6. Answers may vary. Sample answer: (using system in Exercise 5)
$x \approx 6.91$; $y \approx 2.152$

7. Answers may vary. Sample answer: Drink another glass of milk and take a multivitamin.

8. Females: 660 calories
Males: 900 calories

9. 660 calories is equivalent to approximately 73.3 grams of fat. 900 calories is equivalent to 100 grams of fat.

10. $f = 0.65x + 0.94y$

11. Female: $0.65x + 0.94y \leq 24.4$
Male: $0.65x + 0.94y \leq 33.3$

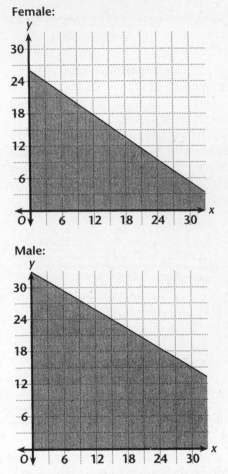

12. Answers may vary. Sample answers: 9 ounces of milk and 8 ounces of cereal. 10.74 grams of fat are left. You can drink low-fat milk to keep fat grams to a minimum.

13. $f = 0.65x + 0.94y + 0.06z$

14. $0.65x + 0.94y + 0.06z \leq 24.4$

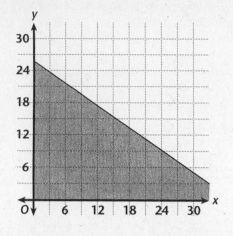

15. Answers may vary. Sample answer: 15 ounces of cereal and 9 ounces of milk

16. Let x represent the number of ounces of lamb and y represent the number of ounces of chocolate ice cream.
$0.62x + 0.26y \geq 8$
$2.27x + 30.90y \leq 200$

17.

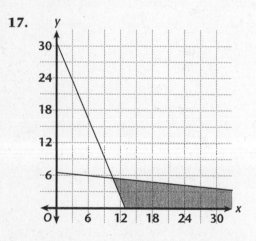

18. $F = 2.61x + 3.12y$

19. The minimum amount of fat will be found at the intersection of the system of equations.
$0.62x + 0.26y = 8$
$2.98x + 30.90y = 200$
which is approximately (10.5, 5.7). The amount of fat will be 45.19 grams.

20. This amount of fat will be over $\frac{1}{3}$ of the daily allowance. You will need to cut back on fat in other meals so that you do not exceed the daily recommended maximum amount of fat.

21. Check students' work.

Long-Term Project — Chapter 4

1. a. $B = [3 \quad 4 \quad 2 \quad 3]$
b. $T = [5 \quad 2 \quad 0 \quad 1]$
c. $G = [0 \quad 5 \quad 4 \quad 0]$
d. $O = [2 \quad 0 \quad 2 \quad 0]$

2. $B + T + G + O = [10 \quad 11 \quad 8 \quad 4]$
The four friends rode the roller coaster a total of 10 times, the bumper cars a total of 11 times, the ferris wheel a total of 8 times, and visited the fun house a total of 4 times.

3. $X = \begin{bmatrix} 3 & 4 & 2 & 3 \\ 5 & 2 & 0 & 1 \\ 0 & 5 & 4 & 0 \\ 2 & 0 & 2 & 0 \end{bmatrix}$

4. $R = \begin{bmatrix} 5 \\ 3 \\ 2 \\ 1 \end{bmatrix}$

5. Since X has dimensions 4×4 and R has dimensions 4×1, the matrices can be multiplied. Matrix XR has dimensions 4×1.

6. $\begin{bmatrix} 34 \\ 32 \\ 23 \\ 14 \end{bmatrix}$

7. a. the number of tickets Brett used
b. the number of tickets Terri used
c. does not exist

8. $2(XR) = \begin{bmatrix} 68 \\ 64 \\ 46 \\ 28 \end{bmatrix}$

9.

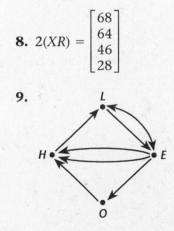

10.

To:
$$\begin{array}{c} & \begin{array}{cccc} L & E & H & O \end{array} \\ \text{From:} \begin{array}{c} L \\ E \\ H \\ O \end{array} & \left[\begin{array}{cccc} 0 & 2 & 0 & 0 \\ 1 & 0 & 2 & 1 \\ 1 & 0 & 0 & 0 \\ 0 & 0 & 1 & 0 \end{array}\right] \end{array}$$

11.

To:
$$\begin{array}{c} & \begin{array}{cccc} L & E & H & O \end{array} \\ \text{From:} \begin{array}{c} L \\ E \\ H \\ O \end{array} & \left[\begin{array}{cccc} 2 & 0 & 4 & 2 \\ 2 & 2 & 1 & 0 \\ 0 & 2 & 0 & 0 \\ 1 & 0 & 0 & 0 \end{array}\right] \end{array}$$

12. 4

13. Since $n_{32} = 2$, there are 2 two-stage paths from the Hall of Mirrors to the Enchanted Forest. Both paths go from the Hall of Mirrors to the Lion's Den to the Enchanted Forest; there are two paths because there are two doors leading from the Lion's Den to the Enchanted Forest.

14. Answers may vary. Sample answer:

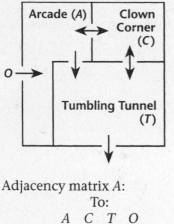

Adjacency matrix A:

To:
$$\begin{array}{c} & \begin{array}{cccc} A & C & T & O \end{array} \\ \text{From:} \begin{array}{c} A \\ C \\ T \\ O \end{array} & \left[\begin{array}{cccc} 0 & 1 & 1 & 0 \\ 1 & 0 & 1 & 0 \\ 0 & 1 & 0 & 1 \\ 1 & 0 & 0 & 0 \end{array}\right] \end{array}$$

2-stage path matrix A^2:

To:
$$\begin{array}{c} & \begin{array}{cccc} A & C & T & O \end{array} \\ \text{From:} \begin{array}{c} A \\ C \\ T \\ O \end{array} & \left[\begin{array}{cccc} 1 & 1 & 1 & 1 \\ 0 & 2 & 1 & 1 \\ 2 & 0 & 1 & 0 \\ 0 & 1 & 1 & 0 \end{array}\right] \end{array}$$

For example, $n_{31} = 2$. This means that there are 2 two-ways paths from the Tumbling Tunnel to the Arcade. They are through the Clown Corner and through the outside.

15. $\begin{cases} 2w + h = 348 \\ w + 2h = 276 \end{cases}$

16. $\begin{bmatrix} 2 & 1 \\ 1 & 2 \end{bmatrix}\begin{bmatrix} w \\ h \end{bmatrix} = \begin{bmatrix} 348 \\ 276 \end{bmatrix}$
$w = 140$ pounds; $h = 68$ inches

17. $\begin{bmatrix} 2 & 1 \\ 1 & 2 \end{bmatrix}\begin{bmatrix} w \\ h \end{bmatrix} = \begin{bmatrix} 313 \\ 251 \end{bmatrix}$
$w = 125$ pounds; $h = 63$ inches

18. $\begin{bmatrix} w \\ h \end{bmatrix} = \begin{bmatrix} 2 & 1 \\ 1 & 2 \end{bmatrix}^{-1}\begin{bmatrix} c \\ d \end{bmatrix}$

19. Let x represent the amount spent by Brett, y represent the amount spent by George, and z represent the amount spent by Ondine.

$x + y + z = 142$
$x = y + z - 6$
$x = 2z + 12$

$$\begin{bmatrix} 1 & 1 & 1 \\ 1 & -1 & -1 \\ 1 & 0 & -2 \end{bmatrix}\begin{bmatrix} x \\ y \\ z \end{bmatrix} = \begin{bmatrix} 142 \\ -6 \\ 12 \end{bmatrix}$$

$$\begin{bmatrix} x \\ y \\ z \end{bmatrix} = \begin{bmatrix} 68 \\ 46 \\ 28 \end{bmatrix}$$

Brett spent \$68, George spent \$46, and Ondine spent \$28.

20. $\left[\begin{array}{ccc|c} 1 & 1 & 1 & 142 \\ 1 & -1 & -1 & -6 \\ 1 & 0 & -2 & 12 \end{array}\right]$

$1R_2 + R_1 \to R_1$ $\left[\begin{array}{ccc|c} 2 & 0 & 0 & 136 \\ 1 & -1 & -1 & -6 \\ 1 & 0 & -2 & 12 \end{array}\right]$

$\frac{1}{2}R_1 \to R_1$ $\left[\begin{array}{ccc|c} 1 & 0 & 0 & 68 \\ 1 & -1 & -1 & -6 \\ 1 & 0 & -2 & 12 \end{array}\right]$

$-1R_1 + R_2 \to R_2$ $\left[\begin{array}{ccc|c} 1 & 0 & 0 & 68 \\ 0 & -1 & -1 & -74 \\ 1 & 0 & -2 & 12 \end{array}\right]$

$-1R_1 + R_3 \to R_3$ $\left[\begin{array}{ccc|c} 1 & 0 & 0 & 68 \\ 0 & -1 & -1 & -74 \\ 0 & 0 & -2 & -56 \end{array}\right]$

ANSWERS

$-1R_2 \rightarrow R_2$
$\begin{bmatrix} 1 & 0 & 0 & | & 68 \\ 0 & 1 & 1 & | & 74 \\ 0 & 0 & -2 & | & -56 \end{bmatrix}$

$-\frac{1}{2}R_3 \rightarrow R_3$
$\begin{bmatrix} 1 & 0 & 0 & | & 68 \\ 0 & 1 & 1 & | & 74 \\ 0 & 0 & 1 & | & 28 \end{bmatrix}$

$-1R_3 + R_2 \rightarrow R_2$
$\begin{bmatrix} 1 & 0 & 0 & | & 68 \\ 0 & 1 & 0 & | & 46 \\ 0 & 0 & 1 & | & 28 \end{bmatrix}$

21. Answers may vary. Sample answer: Elena, Michael, and Tyler spent a total of $64 at an amusement park. Together, Michael and Tyler spent $8 more than Elena. Elena spent twice as much as Tyler.

Let x = amount spent by Elena
y = amount spent by Michael
z = amount spent by Tyler

$x + y + z = 64$
$y + z = x + 8$
$x = 2z$

Solving by inverse matrices:

$\begin{bmatrix} 1 & 1 & 1 \\ -1 & 1 & 1 \\ 1 & 0 & -2 \end{bmatrix}\begin{bmatrix} x \\ y \\ z \end{bmatrix} = \begin{bmatrix} 64 \\ 8 \\ 0 \end{bmatrix}$

$\begin{bmatrix} x \\ y \\ z \end{bmatrix} = \begin{bmatrix} 28 \\ 22 \\ 14 \end{bmatrix}$

Solving by row reduction:

$\begin{bmatrix} 1 & 1 & 1 & | & 64 \\ -1 & 1 & 1 & | & 8 \\ 1 & 0 & -2 & | & 0 \end{bmatrix}$

$-1R_2 + R_1 \rightarrow R_1$
$\begin{bmatrix} 2 & 0 & 0 & | & 56 \\ -1 & 1 & 1 & | & 8 \\ 1 & 0 & -2 & | & 0 \end{bmatrix}$

$\frac{1}{2}R_1 \rightarrow R_1$
$\begin{bmatrix} 1 & 0 & 0 & | & 28 \\ -1 & 1 & 1 & | & 8 \\ 1 & 0 & -2 & | & 0 \end{bmatrix}$

$1R_1 + R_2 \rightarrow R_2$
$\begin{bmatrix} 1 & 0 & 0 & | & 28 \\ 0 & 1 & 1 & | & 36 \\ 1 & 0 & -2 & | & 0 \end{bmatrix}$

$-1R_1 + R_3 \rightarrow R_3$
$\begin{bmatrix} 1 & 0 & 0 & | & 28 \\ 0 & 1 & 1 & | & 36 \\ 0 & 0 & -2 & | & -28 \end{bmatrix}$

$-\frac{1}{2}R_3 \rightarrow R_3$
$\begin{bmatrix} 1 & 0 & 0 & | & 28 \\ 0 & 1 & 1 & | & 36 \\ 0 & 0 & 1 & | & 14 \end{bmatrix}$

$-1R_3 + R_2 \rightarrow R_2$
$\begin{bmatrix} 1 & 0 & 0 & | & 28 \\ 0 & 1 & 0 & | & 22 \\ 0 & 0 & 1 & | & 14 \end{bmatrix}$

Long-Term Projects — Chapter 5

1. The parabola opens down. Explanations may vary. Sample explanation: This makes sense because the rocket rises to maximum altitude, and then descends.

2.

t	0	4	8	12	16
$h(t)$	0	768	1024	768	0

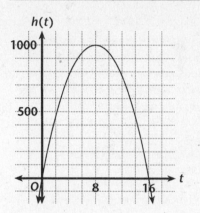

3. Vertex is at (8, 1024); maximum

4. The t-coordinate of the vertex represents the time when the rocket reaches its maximum altitude; the $h(t)$ coordinate represents the height of the maximum altitude.

5. Answers may vary. Sample answer: Negative values for time do not make sense because there is no path before the rocket is launched at $t = 0$. Negative values for height do not make sense because they would indicate that the rocket is traveling below the ground.

6. after ≈ 9.7 seconds

7. The timer should be set for 7.5 seconds. Explanations may vary. Sample explanation: I solved $600 = -16t^2 + 1500$ for t.

ANSWERS

8. Answers may vary. Sample table:

t	0	2.5	5	7.5	10
$h(t)$	1500	1400	1100	600	−100

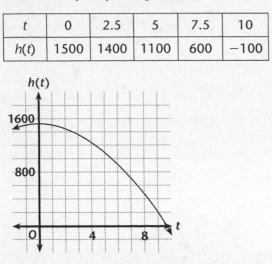

9. Answers may vary. Sample answer: The graph shows that the altitude of the projectile is zero when t is a little less than 10 seconds, confirming the answer to Exercise 6, and that the altitude is 600 feet at $t = 7.5$ seconds, confirming the answer to Exercise 7.

10. $h(t) = -16t^2 + 224t$

11. 0 seconds and 14 seconds

12. The fuse should be set for 7 seconds. Explanations may vary. Sample explanation: The vertex is halfway between the zeros at $t = 0$ and $t = 14$. Maximum altitude occurs at the average of the two elapsed times found.

13. $h(t) = -16t^2 + 144t$

14. $320 = -16t^2 + 144t;\ 0 = -16t^2 + 144t - 320$, or $16t^2 - 144t + 320 = 0$

15. The fuse can be set for either 4 or 5 seconds.

16. a. $0 = -16t^2 + 200t - 450$, or $16t^2 - 200t + 450 = 0$
b. $0 = -16t^2 + 200t - 700$, or $16t^2 - 200t + 700 = 0$

17. The fuse for the third rocket may be set for either $t = 2.9$ or $t = 9.6$ seconds. When you use the quadratic formula to solve for the fourth rocket's fuse times, you find a negative discriminant. This means that there are no real solutions to the equation, so there is no time when the rocket reaches a height of 700 feet.

18. $-16t^2 + 200t \geq 580;\ -16t^2 + 200t - 580 \geq 0$, or $0 \geq 16t^2 - 200t + 580$

19. $-16t^2 + 200t - 580 = 0$, or $0 = 16t^2 - 200t + 580;\ t = 4.6$ seconds or $t = 7.9$ seconds

20. The function represents the altitude of the rocket if it were launched from 580 feet below the surface. The times for which the altitude is positive correspond to the altitudes greater than 580 feet if it were launched at ground level.

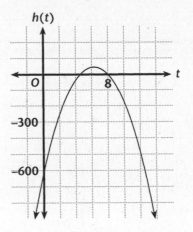

21. The rocket should burst between $t = 4.6$ and $t = 7.9$ seconds ($4.6 \leq t \leq 7.9$). Explanations may vary. Sample explanation: The graph shows that the related function is positive between $t = 4.6$ and $t = 7.9$ seconds.

ANSWERS

22. Answers will vary.
The Screamer must burst between $t = 3.2$ and $t = 6.8$ seconds; it reaches its maximum altitude at $t = 5$ seconds.
Mod Quad must burst between $t = 2.1$ and $t = 10.4$ seconds; it reaches its maximum altitude at $t = 6.25$ seconds.
Newton's Glory must burst between $t = 1.6$ and $t = 13.4$ seconds; it reaches its maximum altitude at $t = 7.5$ seconds.
Sample explanation: Use the quadratic formula to find the times when each rocket reaches an altitude of 350 feet, then choose a time between these times to satisfy the safety requirement. To find the time for the maximum altitude for one of the rockets, average the two times that it was at an altitude of 350 feet. To find the altitudes of the rockets at the times chosen, substitute these times for t into the equations.

23. a. For $h(t) = -16t^2 + v_0 t$, $a = -16$, $b = v_0$, and $c = 0$. The discriminant is $(v_0)^2 - 4(-16)(0) = (v_0)^2 > 0$. Thus, there are two values of t for which $h(t) = 0$.

b. maximum altitude: $\frac{(v_0)^2}{64}$

Long-Term Projects — Chapter 6

Note: Different rounding strategies will result in slightly different answers than the ones given below.

1. $1124.86

2. $1157.63

3. Answers may vary. Sample answer: If you think you may need some or all of the money before the term of the longer-term account is over, you may decide to choose the shorter-term account.

4. a. 7% interest annually

Time	1	2	3
Amount	1070.00	1144.90	1225.04

b. 7% interest semiannually

Time	0.5	1	1.5
Amount	1035	1071.23	1108.72

2	2.5	3
1147.52	1187.69	1229.26

5. None of the investments will be worth $1800 in 3 years or less.

6. for the first stock, $A(t) = 1000(1.19)^t$
for the second stock, $A(t) = 1000(0.91)^t$

7.

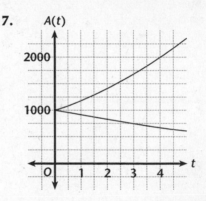

8. The function representing the first stock shows exponential growth; the function representing the second stock shows exponential decay.

9. No; this investment will be worth $1800 in about 3.4 years.

10. about 13.5 years

11. about 29%

12. yes

13. about 123.6%

14. about $11,180

15. It would take less than a year (approximately 8.8 months) before the computer could be bought. Explanations may vary. Sample explanation: I used logarithms to solve $1000 \times (2.236)^t = 1800$. Dividing by 1000 and taking logs of both sides gives $\log 2.236^t = \log 1.8$. This means $t = \dfrac{\log 1.8}{\log 2.236}$.

16. $1072.51; slightly more than 7% compounded annually or semiannually

17. $t \approx 8.4$; this is the number of years it will take the account to accumulate $1800.

18.

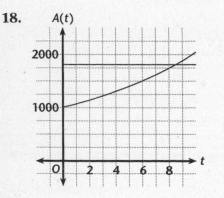

19. Answers may vary. Sample answer: The point of intersection of the graphs occurs between $t = 8$ and $t = 9$, which is consistent with the answer of 8.4 found algebraically.

20. Approximate values are given.

Investment	Doubling time	Time to $1800	Value after 10 years
CD	17.7 years	15.0 years	$1480.24
Investment account	9.9 years	8.4 years	$2013.75
Stock	4.0 years	3.4 years	$5694.68
Collectible toys	1.2 years	1.0 years	$348,911.99

21. Answers may vary. Sample answer: Choose to invest in the stock. The two investments with less risk take too long to earn $1800, and the collectible toys are too risky.

22. Answers may vary. Sample answer: Invest $800 in the investment account and $200 in the collectible toys. That way, most of the money will be safe. The investor will still have a chance to make a lot of money if the collectible toy market continues to skyrocket.

Long-Term Projects — Chapter 7

1. cubic trinomial

2.

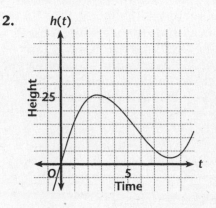

3. Answers may vary. Sample answer: The coaster is at a height of 0 feet at $t = 0$ seconds, which makes sense because it should be at ground level when the ride begins.

4. 2.7 feet

5. Answers may vary. Sample answer: According to this function, the coaster is at a height of 48,060 feet at $t = 60$ seconds, which is impossible. After 10 seconds, the function just keeps increasing, but a roller coaster does not continue increasing in height until the end of the ride.

6. Answers may vary. Sample answer: A quartic function would be the best model, because this section of the graph has 3 turning points.

ANSWERS

7.

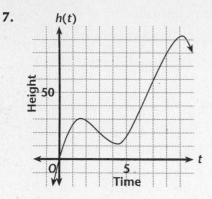

8. maxima at approximately (1.5, 30.5) and (9.2, 92.2), minimum at approximately (4.3, 12.3). These points represent the peaks and valleys of the roller coaster ride.

9. The curve falls on the left and on the right.

10. Answers may vary. Sample answer: No; we have already seen all of the possible local maxima and minima for this function, so the function only decreases after $t = 10$ seconds, which is not what a real-world roller coaster would do. (In fact, at $t = 120$ seconds, $h \approx -3.5 \times 10^7$ feet, which is about 80% of the way to the other side of Earth!)

11. at 8 seconds: 76.8 feet; at 9 seconds: 91.8 feet; at 10 seconds: 80 feet; at 11 seconds: 19.8 feet

12. a. $w(w - 2)(2w) = 2w^3 - 4w^2$
b. $2w^3 - 4w^2 = 150$; $2w^3 - 4w^2 - 150 = 0$
c.

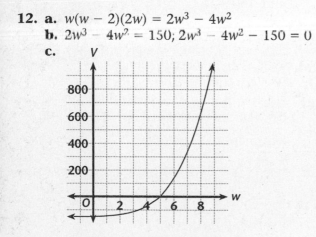

dimensions: width = 5 feet, height = 3 feet, and length = 10 feet

13. $8\pi r^2 + \frac{2}{3}\pi r^3 = \pi r^2\left(8 + \frac{2}{3}r\right)$

14. a. about 3 feet

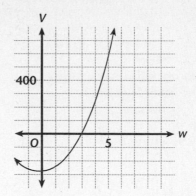

b. The radius hardly changes at all. To the nearest tenth of a foot, the radius stays the same.

15. a.

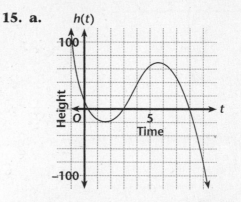

b. Answers may vary. Sample answer: After $t = 8.0$ seconds, the function keeps decreasing, so the model no longer makes sense for a roller coaster. Before $t = 0$ seconds, t has been at very high positive values, which would not make sense for a roller coaster either.
c. The coaster will be 50 feet high at about $t = 4.8$ seconds and $t = 7.1$ seconds.

16. a. $\pm 1, \pm 2, \pm 3, \pm 4, \pm 6, \pm 8, \pm 12, \pm 24, \pm\frac{1}{2},$ $\pm\frac{3}{2}$
b. The zeros are at $t = \frac{1}{2}$, $t = 3$ seconds, and $t = 8$ seconds. These represent the first time the coaster dips below the ground, the first time it emerges, and the second time it dips below the ground, respectively.

17. $h(t) = -\frac{4}{3}t^3 + 24t^2 - \frac{380}{3}t + 200$

ANSWERS

- Algebra - -

Long-Term Projects — Chapter 8

1. a. $s_B = \dfrac{t_A s_A}{t_B}$

   b. $s_B = 195$ revolutions per minute

   c. 16,540.5 inches per minute

   d. about 15.7 miles per hour

2. $t = \dfrac{8}{r}$; inverse variation

3.

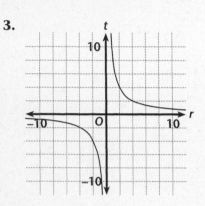

4. domain: $r \neq 0$; in the real world, only positive values of r make sense.

5. $t = \dfrac{8}{r - 4}$

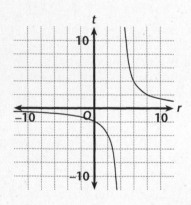

6. $r \neq 4$

7. translated 4 units to the right

8. 1.26 hours; Explanations may vary. Sample explanation: I used $t = \dfrac{8}{r} = \dfrac{8}{15} \approx 0.53$ to find the time for the flat section, then I used $t = \dfrac{8}{r - 4} = \dfrac{8}{11} \approx 0.73$ to find the time for the uphill section. Adding the two times gives the total of 1.26 hours.

9. Simplified expression:
$$\dfrac{s^2 + 111s - 270}{3s(s - 3)} = \dfrac{s^2 + 111s - 270}{3s^2 - 9s}$$
Work shown may vary. Sample of work shown:
$$t = \dfrac{30}{s} + \dfrac{8}{s - 3} + \dfrac{1}{3} = \dfrac{90(s - 3)}{3s^2 - 9s} +$$
$$\dfrac{24s}{3s^2 - 9s} + \dfrac{s^2 - 3s}{3s^2 - 9s} = \dfrac{s^2 + 111s - 270}{3s^2 - 9s}$$

10. speed for flat portion of race = 15 miles per hour; speed for uphill portion = 12 miles per hour

11. Average speed ≈ 15.08 miles per hour; this is not equal to the average of 16.5, 10, and 20; the average speed is not equal to the average of the individual speeds because Chao did not spend the same amount of time riding at each speed.

12. Chao won by about 0.08 hours ≈ 5 minutes. Explanations may vary. Sample explanation: Debbie's time is given to be 3 hours in Exercise 10. By using $t = \dfrac{d}{r}$ for each of Chao's rates given in the table and adding the results, I found Chao's time to be about 2.92 hours, so Chao won the race. She won by $3 - 2.92 = 0.08$ hours; multiplying this by 60 gives the winning margin in minutes.

13. 14 miles

14. $2\sqrt{5} + 4\sqrt{2} \approx 10.13$ miles

15. Barry wins if he rides faster than 11.6 miles per hour; explanations may vary. Sample explanation: Barry's time is $\dfrac{14}{b}$; Evan's time is $\dfrac{10.13}{20 - b}$. If Barry wins, his time is less than Evan's, so $\dfrac{14}{b} < \dfrac{10.13}{20 - b}$. Solving this inequality gives $b > 11.6$.

ANSWERS

16. Answers will vary. Sample answer:

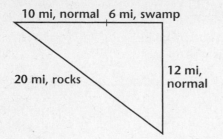

The rider rides 20 miles per hour over normal ground, 16 miles per hour in the swamp, and 10 miles per hour over the rocks. Total time = 3.475 hours; average speed ≈ 13.81 miles per hour

Long-Term Projects — Chapter 9

1. about 93 million miles

2.

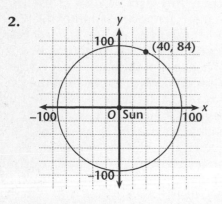

3. $(x - 40)^2 + (y - 84)^2 = 0.24^2 = 0.0576$

4. Earth's orbit encloses about 27,171.63 million square miles; the moon's orbit encloses about 0.18 million square miles; the area enclosed by Earth's orbit is 150,953.5 times greater.

5. $x^2 + y^2 = 67^2 = 4489$

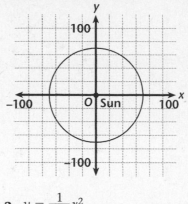

6. a. $y = \frac{1}{240}x^2$

   b. $y = -60$

7. a. aphelion at (43, 0); see graph below.

   b. 72 million miles

   c. (7, 0); see graph below; explanations may vary. Sample explanation: The center is halfway between -29 and 43; the average of -29 and 43 is 7.

   d. $\dfrac{(x - 7)^2}{36^2} + \dfrac{y^2}{35^2} = 1$ or $\dfrac{(x - 7)^2}{1296} + \dfrac{y^2}{1225} = 1$

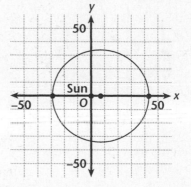

8. Answers may vary. Sample answer: Early astronomers probably believed the orbits were circular, because they did not have instruments sensitive enough to detect the slight variations from circularity.

9. $x^2 + y^2 \approx 7.78$

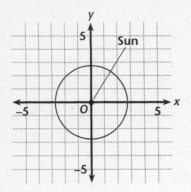

10. **a.** aphelion at (4.57, 0); see graph below.
    b. 7.32 billion miles; (0.91, 0); see graph below.
    c. about 7.1 billion miles
    d. $\dfrac{(x - 0.91)^2}{3.66^2} + \dfrac{y^2}{3.55^2} = 1$
    or $\dfrac{(x - 0.91)^2}{13.40} + \dfrac{y^2}{12.60} = 1$

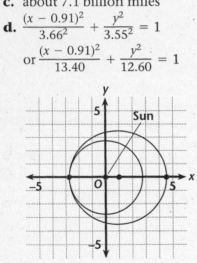

11. Yes; students may believe there are 1 or 2 points of intersection.

12. intersection points at about (−2,59, −1.04), and (−2.59, 1.04); explanations may vary. Sample explanation: I eliminated the y^2 terms by subtracting the equations, then used the quadratic formula to solve the resulting equation. This gave two roots, but only $x \approx -2.59$ made sense. By substituting $x = -2.59$ into the equation for Neptune's orbit, I found that $y \approx \pm 1.04$.

13. No; as shown by the graph and the solution to Exercise 12, Pluto is closer to the Sun than Neptune during part of its orbit. (Pluto was closer to the Sun than Neptune from 1979 to 1999.)

14. An equation is $\dfrac{(x - 83)^2}{100^2} + \dfrac{y^2}{55.78^2} = 1$, or $\dfrac{(x - 83)^2}{10,000} + \dfrac{y^2}{3111} = 1$.

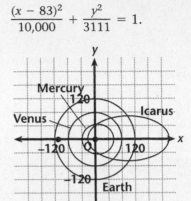

15. Answers may vary. Sample answer: The points of intersection are at approximately (74.6, 55.6) and (74.6, −55.6). The fact that there are points of intersection from this perspective does not mean that Icarus will necessarily collide with Earth. First, the two orbits may not be in the same plane, so the orbits may not actually intersect, like the cars on an overpass crossing over a road below. Even if the orbits did intersect, the Earth and Icarus would have to occupy the same point *at the same time* for a collision to occur.

ANSWERS

Long Term Project — Chapter 10

1. $\frac{7}{21} \approx 33.3\%$

2. There are 30 numbers on the list.

3. 24 different orders

4. 40,320 different orders

5. 293,930 different ways

6. 2002 different ways;
   Explanations may vary. Sample explanation:
   Determine the number of combinations of
   5 players from the 14 players that are left:
   $_{14}C_5 = \frac{14!}{5!(14-5)!} = 2002$

7. 42,336 different teams.
   Explanations may vary. Sample explanation:
   Calculate the following combinations:
   center: $_4C_2 = 6$; forward; $_8C_5 = 56$
   guard $_9C_5 = 126$; find the product of the
   three combinations; $6 \times 56 \times 126 = 42,336$.

8. about 39.7%

9. Yes; Keiko was the only sophomore to try
   out, and 1 sophomore made the varsity
   team, so Keiko made the varsity team.

10. $\frac{18}{21} \approx 85.71\%$

11. $\frac{19}{21} \approx 90.48\%$

12. $\frac{14}{21} \approx 66.67\%$

13. $\frac{1}{7} \cdot \frac{1}{5} = \frac{1}{35} \approx 2.86\%$

14. $\frac{5 \cdot 4 \cdot 3 \cdot 2}{5 \cdot 5 \cdot 5 \cdot 5} = \frac{24}{125} = 19.2\%$

15. $\frac{3}{5} = 60\%$

16. $\frac{3}{7} \approx 42.86\%$

17. $\frac{13}{16} = 81.25\%$; explanations may vary.
    Sample explanation: Redwood was ahead
    at halftime in 16 games, and they won 13
    of those games. So the probability is $\frac{13}{16}$.

18. $\frac{6}{11} \approx 54.55\%$; explanations may vary.
    Sample explanation: Redwood was tied or
    behind at halftime in 6 games, and they
    won 11 of those games. So the probability
    is $\frac{6}{11}$.

19. Answers may vary . Sample answer:

Coin tosses	Tournament (won/lost)
H, T, H, H, T	lost
T, H, T	lost
H, H, H, T, T	lost
H, T, H, H, H	won
T, H, H, T	lost
T, H, T	lost
H, H, T, H, T	lost
H, T, T	lost
H, T, H, H, H	won
T, H, H, T	lost

Based on this simulation, there is a 20%
chance that Redwood will win the
tournament.

20. Answers may vary. Sample answer: 4

ANSWERS

21. Answers may vary. Sample answer: Assign point values as indicated by the roll:
1 to 3: 0 points; 4: 1 point
5 or 6: 2 points; roll the number cube
8 times for each simulation. Repeat 10 times.

Rolls	Points	Win/tie/lose
5, 3, 3, 1, 6, 2, 3, 2	2 + 0 + 0 + 0 + 2 + 0 + 0 + 0 = 4	lose
2, 3, 6, 3, 4, 1, 4, 2	0 + 0 + 2 + 0 + 1 + 0 + 1 + 0 = 4	lose
3, 6, 5, 5, 2, 4, 1, 6	0 + 2 + 2 + 2 + 0 + 1 + 0 + 2 = 9	win
3, 1, 1, 6, 4, 2, 6, 6	0 + 0 + 0 + 2 + 1 + 0 + 2 + 2 = 7	tie
6, 2, 5, 3, 4, 2, 2, 1	2 + 0 + 2 + 0 + 1 + 0 + 0 + 0 = 5	lose
3, 2, 2, 4, 6, 2, 6, 4	0 + 0 + 0 + 1 + 2 + 0 + 2 + 1 = 6	lose
1, 6, 5, 2, 4, 4, 4, 2	0 + 2 + 2 + 0 + 1 + 1 + 1 + 0 = 7	tie
2, 3, 5, 2, 1, 1, 2, 1	0 + 0 + 2 + 0 + 0 + 0 + 0 + 0 = 2	lose
6, 5, 3, 1, 2, 2, 4, 4	2 + 2 + 0 + 0 + 0 + 0 + 1 + 1 = 6	lose
5, 2, 6, 6, 3, 1, 1, 2	2 + 0 + 2 + 2 + 0 + 0 + 0 + 0 = 6	lose

According to this experiment, the probability that Redwood wins or ties is about 30%.

Long-Term Project — Chapter 11

1. 8, 10, 12

2. $t_n = 2n + 6$

3. $t_1 = 8$ and $t_n = t_{n-1} + 2$

4. $t_8 = 2(8) + 6 = 22$
There are 22 seats in the eighth row. Answers may vary. Sample answer: The explicit formula was used because only one calculation was needed. The recursive formula requires 7 calculations to compute the eighth term of the sequence.

5. $t_1 = 8$, $t_9 = 24$, average: 16
The average number of seats in each row is 16.

6. $t_1 = 4(1) + 4 = 8$
$t_2 = 4(2) + 4 = 12$
$t_3 = 4(3) + 4 = 16$
$t_4 = 4(4) + 4 = 20$
$t_5 = 4(5) + 4 = 24$
The numbers of seats in the first 5 rows are 8, 12, 16, 20, 24.

7. $t_1 = 8$, $t_7 = 32$, average: 20
The average number of seats in each row is 20.

8. $\displaystyle\sum_{n=1}^{n}(4n + 4) = 4\sum_{n=1}^{7} n + 4(7)$
$= 4(1 + 2 + 3 + 4 + 5 + 6 + 7) + 28$
$= 4(28) + 28$
$= 140$
Answers may vary. Sample answer: The sum represents the total number of seats in the theater using Option B.

9. $\displaystyle\sum_{n=1}^{9}(2n + 6) = 2\sum_{n=1}^{9} n + 9(6)$
$= 2(1 + 2 + 3 + 4 + 5 + 6 + 7 + 8 + 9) + 54$
$= 2(45) + 54$
$= 144$
The seating capacity for Option A is 144 seats. Explanations may vary. Sample explanation: Take the explicit formula for the number of seats in the nth row and find the sum of the number of seats in the rows using the fact that there are 9 rows.

10. Option A seats more people. Seats are farther from the stage in Option A because it has 2 more rows than Option B. Answers may vary. Sample answer: Choose Option B because there are only 4 fewer seats and no seat is more than 7 rows away from the stage.

11. 24 seats

12. $\dfrac{24}{16} = \dfrac{3}{2}$

13. $t_n = 16\left(\dfrac{3}{2}\right)^{n-1}$
Explanations may vary. Sample explanation: The sequence is a geometric sequence whose first term is 16 and whose constant ratio is $\dfrac{3}{2}$.

14. $t_4 = 16\left(\frac{3}{2}\right)^{4-1} = 16\left(\frac{3}{2}\right)^3 = 16\left(\frac{27}{8}\right) = 54$

15. Answers may vary. Sample answer:
There can be the same number of seats on each side of the stage (27) but not on each side of the aisle. Arrange the seats so that there are 13 seats, then the aisle, then 14 seats. Have the side with 13 seats face the side with 13 seats on the other side of the stage (so the sides with 14 seats are also facing each other).

16. $\sum_{n=1}^{4} 16\left(\frac{3}{2}\right)^{n-1}$

$= 16\left[\left(\frac{3}{2}\right)^0 + \left(\frac{3}{2}\right)^1 + \left(\frac{3}{2}\right)^2 + \left(\frac{3}{2}\right)^3\right]$

$= 16\left[1 + \frac{3}{2} + \frac{9}{4} + \frac{27}{8}\right]$

$= 16\left[\frac{8}{8} + \frac{12}{8} + \frac{18}{8} + \frac{27}{8}\right]$

$= 16\left[\frac{65}{8}\right]$

$= 130$

Yes, this design seats at least 125 people.

17. Answers may vary. Sample answer:
Option A: This design seats the greatest number of people (144), but contains the greatest number of rows (9). The largest number of seats in any row is 24, with 12 seats on either side of the aisle.
Option B: This design is in the middle in terms of both seating capacity (140) and number of rows (7). The largest number of seats in any row is 32, with 16 seats on either side of the aisle.
Option C: This design seats the fewest people (130) in the fewest rows (4). The largest number of seats in any row is 54, but this is divided into 4 parts, with 13 or 14 seats in each. This design has the possible disadvantage of half of the audience being behind the actors; however, this could lead to more creative direction and innovative feeling.
Recommendation: Option A seems to be the best design. It accommodates the largest number of people without too large a number of rows, and it keeps the number of seats per row to a reasonable amount.

18. $t_n = t_1 r^{n-1}$
$5.12 = (12.50)r^{5-1}$
$\pm 0.8 = r$
$t_1 = 12.50;\ t_2 = 10.00;\ t_3 = 8.00;$
$t_4 = 6.40;\ t_5 = 5.12$
The three positive geometric means are 10, 8, and 6.4. These numbers represent the prices of tickets in Row 2, Row 3, and Row 4, respectively.

19. a. about 34.4%
b. Explanations may vary. Sample explanation: Find $\frac{_6C_6}{2^6} + \frac{_6C_5}{2^6} + \frac{_6C_4}{2^6}$.

20. about 42.4%

21. Answers may vary. Sample answer:

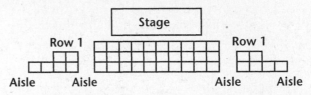

The seating plan follows an arithmetic sequence, with $t_n = 4n + 6$. There are 7 rows, for a total seating capacity of 154. Ticket prices follow an arithmetic sequence, where $d = \$2.50$, so $t_1 = \$25$, $t_2 = \$22.50$, $t_3 = \$20.00$, $t_4 = \$17.50$, $t_5 = \$15.00$, $t_6 = \$12.50$ and $t_7 = \$10.00$.

Long-Term Projects — Chapter 12

1.

Rank	Earnings per screen (thousands of dollars)
1	13.995
2	9.673
3	7.969
4	6.730
5	4.936
6	5.542
7	4.168
8	4.005
9	3.575
10	2.661

ANSWERS

2. mean: $15,460,000; median: $11,650,000; Explanations may vary. Sample explanation: There is no mode because no amount appears more than once in the data set.

3. mean: $6325; median: $5239

4. Answers may vary. Sample answer: Suggest $6325 per week. Choose the mean because the manager wants an estimate of the *annual* revenue that will result from running a top-ten movie on a screen every week, and the mean (multiplied by 52) provides the best estimate of this quantity.

5. earnings per screen: $27,989; mean: $7725; median: $5239. Answers may vary. Sample answer: I would not change my estimate, because this behavior is probably not typical. The new data point is most likely an outlier.

6.

Stem	Leaf	1|0 = 10
0	1 1 1 2 2 2 3 4 4 5 6 6 7	
1	0 0 2 4 5	
2	0 1	

7. 146; 82

8. Answers may vary. Sample answer: Choose movie magazines, since frequent moviegoers buy more tickets, but the final decision would depend on other factors, such as the cost of advertising and the number of people who would see each type of advertisement.

9.

Amount Spent	Frequency
1	1
2	3
3	3
4	5
5	3
6	4
7	7
8	7
9	3
10	2
11	1
12	1

10.

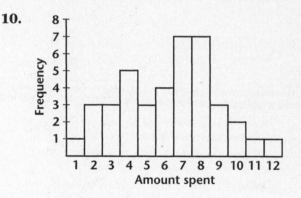

11. quartiles: $Q_1 = 4$, $Q_2 = 7$, $Q_3 = 8$; range: 11; interquartile range: 4; no outliers

12. quartiles: $Q_1 = 3$, $Q_2 = 5$, $Q_3 = 6$; range: 11; interquartile range: 3; 12 is an outlier.

13.

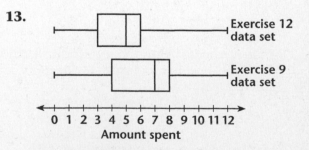

14. Answers may vary. Sample answer: It appears that most people spend more money at noon on Saturday than at 9:00 P.M. on Tuesday. Perhaps people are hungrier at this time.

15. Ex 9: $\sigma \approx 2.624$; Ex 12: $\sigma \approx 2.261$; descriptions may vary. Sample description: The data set in Exercise 12 is more consistent.

16. 0.112, or 11.2%

17. 0.263, or 26.3%

18. Answers may vary. Sample answer: 30%; 0.472, or 47.2%

19. Answers may vary. Students should answer "yes" if they chose a percentage of 31.4% or above in Exercise 18.

20. 0.683, or 68.3%

21. 0.428, or 42.8%

22. 0.196, or 19.6%

23. Answers may vary. Sample answer: Survey 10 students in the class to find out how many movies they went to last year. Data might be: 18, 4, 6, 24, 3, 6, 11, 16, 35, 28. The mean is 15.1, the median is 13.5, the mode is 6, and the standard deviation is about 10.5. A stem-and-leaf plot and box-and-whisker plot are shown below.

Stem	Leaf
0	3 4 6 6
1	1 6 8
2	4 8
3	5

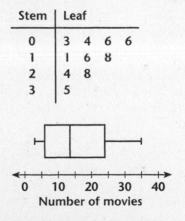

Number of movies

Long Term Projects — Chapter 13

1. $m\angle C \approx 56.8°$; $m\angle B \approx 33.2°$; $a \approx 31.1$ miles

2. about 53.1° to the left; explanations may vary. Possible explanation:

$\tan \theta = \dfrac{y}{x} = \dfrac{8}{6} = \dfrac{4}{3}$, so

either $\theta = \tan^{-1} \dfrac{4}{3} \approx 53.1°$ or

$\theta = 180° + \tan^{-1} \dfrac{4}{3} \approx 223.1°$.

Note that 53.1° is in the correct quadrant.

3. 120°

4. $\theta_{\text{ref}} = 60°$; $\sin \theta = \dfrac{\sqrt{3}}{2}$; $\cos \theta = -\dfrac{1}{2}$;

$\tan \theta = -\sqrt{3}$; $\csc \theta = \dfrac{2\sqrt{3}}{3}$; $\sec \theta = -2$;

$\cot \theta = -\dfrac{\sqrt{3}}{3}$

5. $\dfrac{\pi}{60}$ radians per second; 3° per second

6. $\dfrac{\pi}{6}$ centimeters per second

7. about $(-3.7, -9.3)$

8. 68° to the left; explanations will vary. Possible explanation: $248° - 180° = 68°$. The Doubloon should turn 68° to obtain a new heading directly opposite Captain O'Mean.

9. about 457.4 meters

10. a. amplitude: 1.6; period: 12; phase shift: 4; vertical translation: 0

b.
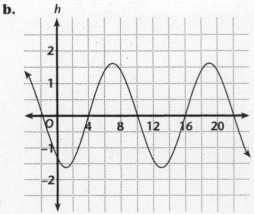

11. 7:00 A.M. and 7:00 P.M.

12. 1:00 A.M. and 1:00 P.M.

ANSWERS

13. **a.** about $(-22.3, 20.1)$; explanations may vary. Possible explanation: $30 \cos 138° \approx -22.3$ and $30 \sin 138° \approx 20.1$.
   b. No
   c. No, the correct angle is about $132.0°$. Explanations may vary. Possible
   explanation: $\tan \theta = \dfrac{y}{x} = -\dfrac{10}{9}$, so either
   $\theta = \tan^{-1}\left(-\dfrac{10}{9}\right) \approx -48°$ or
   $\theta = 180° + \tan^{-1}\left(-\dfrac{10}{9}\right) \approx 132.0°$.
   Note that $132.0°$ is in the correct quadrant.
   d. No, the correct length is about 13.5 centimeters. Explanations may vary. Possible explanation:
   $r = \sqrt{x^2 + y^2} = \sqrt{(-9)^2 + 10^2}$
   $= \sqrt{181} \approx 13.5$ centimeters

14. **a.** $r \approx 33.0$ centimeters; $\theta \approx 55.0°$
   b. $r \approx 14.4$ centimeters; $\theta \approx 146.3°$
   c. $r \approx 23.4$ centimeters; $\theta \approx 312.4°$

15. $\overline{PQ}$: 7.6 nautical miles at $66.8°$;
   $\overline{QR}$: 8.2 nautical miles at $14.0°$;
   $\overline{RS}$: 7.8 nautical miles at $39.8°$;
   $\overline{ST}$: 7.2 nautical miles at $-56.3°$

Long-Term Projects — Chapter 14

1. about 36.7 square miles

2. **a.** 1.226 kilometers, or 1226 meters
   b. 703 meters; explanations may vary. Sample explanation: Solving $h = 1226 \sin 35°$ gives $h = 703$.

3. 0.6 kilometers; law of cosines

4. 4.0 kilometers

5. $0.8\overline{3} \approx 0.8$ hours, or exactly 50 minutes

6. **a.** $6.8°$
   b. $8.5°$
   c. 0.12; explanations may vary. Sample explanation: The wax with this coefficient needs a smaller angle to overcome friction.

7. $m\angle A \approx 14.7°$, $m\angle DBC \approx 20.9°$

8. **a.** $\begin{bmatrix} \dfrac{1}{2} & -\dfrac{\sqrt{3}}{2} \\ \dfrac{\sqrt{3}}{2} & \dfrac{1}{2} \end{bmatrix}$
   b. $(6, 10.4)$
   c. $\begin{bmatrix} -\dfrac{1}{2} & -\dfrac{\sqrt{3}}{2} \\ \dfrac{\sqrt{3}}{2} & -\dfrac{1}{2} \end{bmatrix}$
   d. $(-12, 0)$; explanations may vary. Sample explanation: If a point at $(12, 0)$ is rotated $180°$ about the origin, its final position is $(-12, 0)$.

9. **a.**
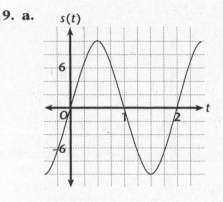
   b. $8 = 10 \sin \pi t$
   c. 0.3 seconds and 0.7 seconds

10. **a.** $17°$
    b. 121.9 meters

11. **a.** From March 6 through October 29
    b. From June 5 through July 30; explanations may vary. Sample explanation: For these dates, $d(t) \leq 0$.

12. 1868 meters; processes may vary. Sample process: The sum of the angle measures for a triangle is $180°$, so $m\angle QRS = 180° - 29° - 18° = 133°$. Since $\angle RQS$ and $\angle PQR$ are supplementary, $m\angle PQR = 180° - 29° = 151°$. By the law of sines, $\dfrac{RQ}{\sin 18°} = \dfrac{4000}{\sin 133°}$, so $RQ \approx 1690.1$ m. By the law of cosines, $RP^2 = 200^2 + 1690.1^2 - 2(200)(1690.1) \cos 151°$, so $RP \approx 1868$ meters.